Mrs. Starkey's
NANNY MANAGER

*The Key to a Successful Relationship
for the Nanny and the Family*

Mrs. Starkey's
NANNY MANAGER

The Key to a Successful Relationship for the Nanny and the Family

Created by

STARKEY
INTERNATIONAL
Denver Colorado

Published by Starkey International Institute for Household Management, Inc.
1350 Logan Street
Denver, CO 80203

The system described in this manual is protected by one or more U.S. Patent applications.

For information about this text or the material within, contact the publisher at:
Phone: (303) 832-5510
Fax: (303) 832-5015
Email: nannyinfo@starkeyintl.com

Publisher's Cataloging-in-Publication Data
International, Starkey.
     Mrs. starkey's nanny manager: the key to a successful relationship for the nanny and the family / Starkey International -- Denver, CO : Starkey International Institute for Household Management, Inc. 1999.
        p. ill. cm.
     Includes index.
     ISBN 0-9664807-0-8
     1. Nanny management. 2. Household staff training. I. Title.
HV7911.N3 A3   1999   98-96272
363.2' 092   dc—21   CIP

PROJECT COORDINATION BY JENKINS GROUP, INC.

03 02 01 00 ◆ 5 4 3 2 1

Printed in the United States of America

Every challenge can teach us something about ourselves.

To be open to this learning is the beginning of success.

ACKNOWLEDGMENTS

The Nanny industry is in the midst of change. The nomination of Zoe Baird to the Office of Attorney General and the subsequent investigation into her personal life brought awareness of the Nanny industry and its use of undocumented workers. The tragedy involving Au Pair Louise Woodward again brought some understanding of what can happen when young women are given too much responsibility without the necessary supervision and support. Working within this industry has encouraged us and directed us to share the knowledge we have learned. This book is not about child development techniques; rather it sets up the service of childcare in your home.

My thanks to John Hookey, Certified HM and Starkey graduate, for his wonderful illustrations of Nannies and children, from the past and present.

My thanks to Lize Csrnko, Laurie Russell, and to Nanny Managers Debbie Bennett and Elizabeth Decker for their editing and ideas. I also want to thank Nanny Manager Jennifer Mendelson for her international travel tips. I wish to express special thanks to Richard Oppenheim and to all of my staff over these last 18 years for their love and support for the Starkey vision. Finally, I wish to extend my deep appreciation to my Starkey Star Nannies and their employers for their continuing belief in Starkey.

Partial proceeds from this book will be donated to benefit burned children through the Zach Foundation.

STARKEY INTERNATIONAL
Setting Standards in Household Service

Our Vision

Starkey International Institute for Household Management is deeply committed to meeting the needs of industry household professionals and of our clients, their employers. Our vision is:

To create and serve a world-recognized personal service industry, in which household service is seen as an art form, where continuing education and growth are valued and standards of professionalism are recognized, honored and required.

Our Starkey Stars, Estate Managers, Household Managers, Nannies, Couples and Chefs are career-minded professionals who have chosen service. They want to make a difference in the lives of those they serve. Our client/employers stand apart from the crowd. They "want it all": a well-nurtured, interactive family, a state-of-the-art, well-maintained home and genuine service relationships that reflect the personality of their home and family. They want to experience a quality of life that matches their lifestyle and service standards. Meeting the employer's standards of excellence is our mission.

Our Services

To meet these standards of service excellence, the Starkey International Institute for Household Management has established:

☆ A training institute, Starkey International Institute for Household Management, to educate our students and employers about standards of service, the **Starkey Household Management System**, the **Nanny Management System** and other household service products. The Institute offers sophisticated and advanced training in professional Household Management for qualified applicants and employers, and a continuing education program for Nannies.

☆ A placement consulting service which matches our Household Managers and Nanny Manager graduates and other experienced industry professionals with qualified employers.

☆ Educational publications and products for the marketplace, including: **Setting Household Standards** (for the Employer), and **The Household Manager's Software**. We also offer **Mrs. Starkey's Nanny Manager** (with Workbook Forms), **Entertaining and The Ballet of Service**, and **Household Culinary Arts and Private Service**. Starkey also publishes quarterly newsletters, **Starkey Stars** for the employer and **Tales from the Mansion** for the professional employee.

☆ **Private Household Service Training** and **On Site Consultations** for developing service standards and a superior service delivery in Household Management, or service delivery and care for children in Nannying. These services are conducted in employers' homes by Mrs. Starkey and other members of the Household Management instruction staff.

Contacting us:

For information about Starkey International services call 1-877-STARKEY.
Or check our web site: www.starkeyinternational.com

CONTENTS

Day in the Life Schedules — 87

Creating a Service Culture — 95

Additional Workbook Forms — 103

PREFACE

If you are a parent who wants the highest level of care for your family, this could be the most important guide you have ever read. If you are a career Nanny wanting to experience your full professional potential, **Mrs. Starkey's Nanny Manager** is a comprehensive summary of all the information and household data you need to set up a successful career path in Nannying.

The idea for building a systematic approach to Nannying originated from our many veteran Nannies, both British and American, who agreed that some structure was essential for success. It was also a result of the challenge of two decades of placing and, more recently, training Nannies for placement in homes throughout the United States. If the placement did not work, Starkey was notified and payment was not received. Our survival, therefore, required us to create successful matches.

This workbook is for parents and professional, career-oriented Nannies. Its primary purpose is to present the **Starkey Nanny Management System**. The Nanny Management System is one application of the **Starkey Household Management System** that is currently being utilized to set up households across the United States and Canada. This communication tool builds a *framework* or *blueprint* for service delivery to take place for the employer, the Nanny and the children. It paints a picture of how to promote a successful relationship between the Nanny and the parents for the care of the children. It aids in creating clear communication between employers and Nannies, and helps them to mutually decide how to manage the Nanny's time. This system adapts to any family, all service standards, all children, any home, and any position requirements.

The Nanny Management System introduces new terminology, such as **Service Standards** and **Day in the Life,** that help build professionalism. It also provides accurate information for both long-term and short-term planning, a way to structure family favorites in logical order, and a system to identify priorities for any family. This streamlined approach takes the Nanny/parent relationship to new heights of professionalism, and injects excitement and self-esteem into the Nanny role. Employers will feel a sense of ownership and gain an understanding of the challenges the Nanny faces in an everyday working schedule.

The Starkey System directs time and energy toward the productive aspects of the Nanny/parent relationship and emphasizes the things that make a difference in the life of the child, and the family as a whole. When Nanny and parents are "on the same page" and working for the same clear, realistic goals, all parties in this important and delicate relationship will feel happier and more secure. Ultimately, we must not forget that the child is the one who will reap the greatest benefits from the stability and consistency of a healthy professional relationship between the parents and the Nanny.

Mrs. Starkey's
NANNY MANAGER

*The Key to a Successful Relationship
for the Nanny and the Family*

Historical Introduction

Perceptions of how childcare "should be" are handed down through generations, within families and cultures. In the education of service providers, Household Managers and Nannies, Starkey International Institute for Household Management finds it most helpful for students and employers to become aware and understand what these perceptions are and how they affect us in the present day. Our past influences how we think about our children, our Nannies and ourselves. This historical reference is taken in part from *The Rise and Fall of the British Nanny* by Jonathan Gathorne-Hardy, and in part from *Serving Women: Household Service in Nineteenth-Century America* by Faye E. Dudden. It will help you to understand the attitudes that have evolved over the centuries in regards to our children, and toward those who are helping us care for them, our Nannies.

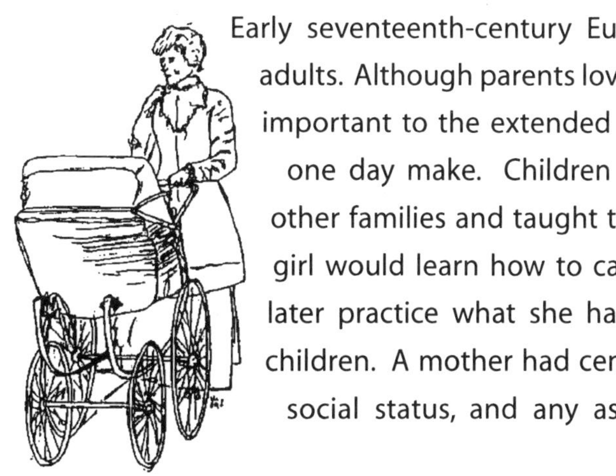

Early seventeenth-century Europeans believed children were miniature adults. Although parents loved their children, primarily the children were important to the extended family because of the alliances they would one day make. Children were commonly fostered out or raised by other families and taught their duties there. This included childcare. A girl would learn how to care for children from her foster mother and later practice what she had been taught on her children and foster children. A mother had central control over her children, whatever her social status, and any assistants, wet nurses, etc., were under the mother's orders and subject to her scrutiny. Harsh and regular beatings were often advocated to correct children of childish behaviors. This attitude was reinforced as Puritan ideas gained strength, because in that strict theology, children who misbehaved were *sinning*, rather than simply making mistakes. Therefore any form of correction, however brutal, was seen as justifiable: it was not only for the good of their socialization, but also for the good of their souls.

In 1692 Locke published a treatise on education, postulating that some childhood behaviors were natural to the condition of childhood and should not be punished, as they would disappear with maturity. In 1762 Rousseau claimed that children were in a state of innocent savagery. Throughout the seventeenth and eighteenth centuries, children started to be seen as children, not as defective adults who had to be brought up to standard.

Friederich Foebel started his first Kindergarten in 1837 with theory based loosely on Locke and Rousseau. The ideas reached England about 1874, and in 1876 Miss Emily Lord opened a school to train teachers along these principles. Later she realized that many of the teachers she was training would make excellent Nannies. She opened the first Nanny training college in 1892, the Norland Nursing School. This was also run along Froebel's lines, and Norland nurses were forbidden to use any corporal punishment whatsoever, which was still quite an enlightened view for the time.

In Great Britain, the very wealthy had always had separate rooms for their children. In the 1800s, as the numbers of the affluent increased, the nursery emerged in more and more homes. In the beginning of the nineteenth century the stereotypical nursery emerged, separating the children physically from the rest of the household. Sometimes the nursery was located in an unpleasant area of the house that was filled with castoff furniture, and sometimes it was in quite a pleasant and cozy area — but it was always separate. The nursery often doubled as a school room. It was also during the 1800s that the affluent mother's control over her children was relinquished and given to hired attendants. She might see them for an hour or so every day, but they were not an important part of her life, nor she of theirs. Two factors which contributed to the rise of the Nanny in the nineteenth century were the decreases in infant mortality and the wealth created by the

Industrial Revolution. Once the *average* became five or six children per family, those families with sufficient means to do so would hire attendants for their children. The average number of children was probably higher among the wealthy, thereby creating a huge demand for Nannies.

Since this was during Victorian times, when hierarchy was paramount, the Nanny reigned supreme in her sphere of the nursery. She derived her authority from the lady of the house and exercised it over the children and nursery-maids (usually one per child). The duties, clothing, training, etc. of the Nanny were defined between 1850 and 1880. Prior to 1850, she had been a child's nurse, but the gradual change to a Nanny was codified during this time. The nursery-maids were the liaisons with the rest of the household, while the Nanny kept her charges insulated from much of their parents' doings, oftentimes serving as such a buffer that children were completely unaware of any marital discord between their parents, and in the event of a divorce, it scarcely registered. Most often it seems that the Nanny completely dominated the upbringing of the children, not allowing parents to "interfere." Politically and geographically, the children were the Nanny's domain.

Another impact of the hierarchical mind-set was that the Nanny preserved class distinctions. She might have been in charge of upper-class children, but she was a servant. Caring for these children was seen, therefore, as a function of the lower and working classes, just as caring for anything else of the wealthy was. The actual mothers of these children often had no idea how to cope with their children, and further thought that this was not their function, but that of the laboring class.

Nanny training was traditionally provided by Nannies. Even after the first school for Nannies opened in 1892, the proportion of Nannies who were trained in that way was negligible. The system of a nursery presided over by a Nanny and using several nursery-maids served as an apprenticeship system. Eventually a nursery-maid would be ready to assume Nanny status, and she would move on to a different family who needed her in that position. Interestingly, even Nannies who were themselves trained at a school continued the apprenticeship system by training others. Nannies generally wore uniforms that were recognized by all as Nanny uniforms, though the variations of Nanny costume were numerous. Nannies trained at a particular school wore uniforms indicating, by color or style, that they had gone to that school. The Nannies trained by these graduates wore variations of the style of the trainer's alma mater!

The American Nanny Industry is still in its infancy. Early childcare providers were either part of the extended family (unmarried aunts or nieces) or were brought over to this country as indentured servants or slaves. At the beginning of World War II, the American government opened up day-care centers to care for the nation's children so that mothers could go into the factories and businesses to keep the economy working. When the war ended, so did the day-care centers, as American women were expected to return home to care for their own children. In the 1960s, when mothers of all economic backgrounds began to enter the work force, the need for child and household care began to grow.

In 1987, I (*Mary Starkey*) was one of approximately fifteen agency owners, childcare educators and Nannies who came together and formed the International Nanny Association. Long hours were spent discussing what to call America's new at-home childcare provider. A decision was made to borrow from the British their professional childcare terminology, and the Professional American Nanny was named! The Nanny Industry, as a profession in America, was officially born. Starkey & Associates, Inc. hosted the nation's first international Nanny conference in 1988 in Vail, Colorado. Three hundred Nannies, educators, school owners, and Nanny placement agencies came together to begin the work of defining terms, articulating standards, and honoring exceptional childcare work. The conference hosted representatives from the U.S., Canada, England, Scotland, and Ireland.

At this gathering it was recognized that the tradition of childcare in private homes is not always valued. Some parents feel guilty about leaving their children in another's charge. Formal child-development education is rarely required in most homes. Many families are challenged by the cost of employing a Nanny, training and managing the service delivery, and the Nanny's lack of under-standing of how to live and work in another's home. American society does not honor professional childcare providers of any type, and Nannies, in particular, suffer from being associated with the servants or slaves of the past or the illegal aliens of today. Most Nannies struggle with the perception that their work is neither difficult nor valuable, and because of the resulting low self-esteem, they allow themselves to be subjected to low pay, do not expect to receive benefits or to have their taxes paid by the employer as "real" employees would. They work long hours, are frequently on-call and feel they have poor communication with their employers.

The conference was a good start, but the Nanny Industry has yet to organize or professionalize fully. There are, however, regional Nanny groups which support the emotional and educational needs of Nannies. In the early 1990s there were as many as twenty-five Nanny training schools, but today there are only a few.

Our marketplace can use the term "Nanny" to describe any of the following:

☆ A British Nanny

☆ An undocumented worker

☆ An Au Pair

☆ A young American girl, trained or untrained

☆ A middle-aged woman, trained and highly educated

☆ An older woman, educated and experienced, having reared her own children

The Nanny Placement Agents, who recruit and place, see a great demand for qualified Nannies. They experience the rage and sometimes the legal proceedings of parents when Nannies do not work out; they continue to work hard to recruit and to help develop standards within the industry. Few agencies survive the business challenges of what it actually takes to provide this service.

Fortunately, our high schools and community colleges have begun to do a better job of training people to care for children by teaching child-development methodologies. Starkey International has created **Mrs. Starkey's Nanny Manager** to address the continuing education needs of all Career Nannies and Nanny employers.

THE NANNY PROFESSION

Starkey has learned that Service is a Relationship. Nannying is a service that requires a relationship of professionalism, mutual commitment and consistent, excellent communication.

For most industry veterans, Household Service is considered a way of life, a commitment to making a difference in another's life. Nannying, in particular, is seen by most individuals as childcare which happens to be provided within the home setting. However, the true intrinsic value and art form of the Nanny profession lies in the ability to interact with the children in a household in a fashion that wholly supports the values and beliefs — the agenda — of the parents. This does not necessarily mean that parents know all things about raising children, as in many instances a trained and experienced Nanny will have more detailed knowledge, not to mention experience than the parents. Being on the agenda of the parents simply means that the structure for all decisions about raising children must come from the paradigms of the parents. A Nanny must know and follow those paradigms if a successful relationship is to be maintained.

Determining what is contained in those perceptions/paradigms is the crux of what needs to happen before a Nanny can feel secure in charting an action plan and delivering the "Nanny Service" of high-quality, custom-tailored childcare, and before the parents can feel secure in letting the Nanny go ahead and do it. An illustration of how this works can be likened to the manner in which a piece of artwork might be created. First there is an empty canvas. Then the artist(s) adds a form for the purpose of providing a rough sketch, and finally, the finishing colors and textures are added to complete the effort. Using this illustration, we can describe a Nanny who starts a new position (blank canvas), the parents indicate the format (rough sketch), and the Nanny adds the colors and tones (finished art). If the Nanny paints within the rough sketch and uses colors and tones acceptable to the artistic tastes of the parents, all is well and they work in an artistic partnership.

But what happens when the partnership doesn't work? What happens when a Nanny doesn't understand, or decides, for example, to change the outline of the rough sketch? Perhaps the image presented doesn't seem quite right to the Nanny and they decide to paint a different image, one more like another mother may have painted. When the Nanny changes the parents' format (sketch) the risk is substantial. This can jeopardize both the professionalism and the partnership.

This example can also be expanded to include another common scenario. What happens when the Nanny decides to use the color tangerine to paint the pine tree the parents sketched? Probably nothing — unless the parents prefer *tradition* in their artwork! Format is never created by the Nanny, always by the parents. Once the desired end result is specified or sketched out, the parents identify the acceptable and unacceptable procedures for completing the painting.

Some parents may not be clear about their formats or goals, but all parents have them, even if they are not able to articulate them! Parents and Nannies will ideally cooperate on delineating what standards are desired. If the parents fail to make their standards clear, and the Nanny fails to meet the standards, the relationship will typically fail. The Nanny will need to find another position and the family will need to find another Nanny.

Theoretically, a family could eventually find a Nanny whose service standards matched theirs exactly, without any need to discuss how often Junior's sheets are to be changed or what he should and should not eat. Theoretically, a Nanny could eventually work for a family who finds everything to be exactly what they would have chosen, without the tedium of telling or training. This rarely happens by chance. In the short lifetimes which we are provided, it is simpler and more direct for parents to communicate how they want childcare to be provided within their home, and for the Nanny to adjust to their style, respectfully disagree and negotiate something mutually acceptable, or simply decline/resign the position if there is no basic agreement on childcare goals.

What's the point of emphasizing this apparently simple principle? **Mrs. Starkey's Nanny Manager** teaches a Nanny Management System. The system opens up possibilities and helps both Nannies and parents understand what the family values are, what they want for their children, how they want their children punished for inappropriate behavior and rewarded for good behavior. Once the information is organized, it will show how to put a working structure in place to support the family's goals and preferred methods.

Working as a Nanny really means being *support staff.* The term *support staff* implies understanding of and agreement with the concepts one is supporting. A Nanny is not the "owner" and does not share in or own any piece of the "company." Successful Nannies understand that they are *about,* but not *in* the family.

After two decades of talking with childcare professionals, Nannies, and with parents, we have heard several themes repeated many times. In their repetition, they have helped us to define some of the important aspects of being a Nanny. The things that seem to be an integral part of a Nanny's success are simple, but they are not easy.

WHAT WORKS!

The Nanny needs to understand what it means to be employed as a professional.

If you were hiring yourself as a professional, what would you expect to get for your investment? Very few people take the time to put a structure around that concept. Essentially, Nannies must take control of their own jobs and set up a household structure that supports the parents' priorities, a framework within which those priorities can be carried out, and a communication system to report progress to the employer. This is the Nanny Management System. This system also places a value on the person performing those tasks.

The parents need to understand what it means to be an employer.

☆ What is advantageous about working for you and your family to attract a top-notch Nanny?

☆ What is expected in return for the money and benefits paid to the Nanny?

☆ Has a professional employment position been created?

☆ Are extra hours compensated?

☆ How long is the average work day?

☆ Is the Nanny supported in creating a new life within a new geographic community?

☆ Do the living quarters allow a separate personal life away from the family?

☆ Do your management techniques support a Nanny in being successful?

☆ Does your management style challenge a Nanny to become a better Nanny?

The Nanny, rather than a housekeeper, should clean and maintain the children's living area.

This means that Nannies need to know more than child development. Nannies should:

☆ help children learn how to take care of their belongings

☆ sanitize toys and equipment

☆ rotate games, toys and play equipment in the play areas

☆ check for needed repairs on any equipment

☆ organize closets

☆ rotate seasonal clothes and remove old clothes and outgrown equipment

☆ locate missing library books or whatever else has been lost

This list goes on. Nannies say that a great deal about a child's growth and development (socially, academically, spiritually, and physically) is reflected in the "stuff" that they keep in their quarters:

☆ mementos that children collect, such as rocks or bugs or small animals, both stuffed and real

☆ children also save notes and drawings, posters and pictures, treasured toys, awards, preferred blankets or clothing that are very important to them, often for many years

This "stuff" provides loud messages for those who are paying attention. The Nanny had better be paying close attention!

Nannies are role models for their charges.

This means that how the Nanny handles herself, what and how she thinks about herself, her personal ethics and etiquette, her relationship with her employers, and more, all influence the children in her charge. Children also watch how their parents and their parents' friends treat the Nanny. They will most often follow their lead.

NANNIES AND HOUSEHOLD STAFF

Working in a staffed household is very different from other Nanny positions.

In households where there is no staff other than possibly a weekly housekeeper, the Nanny gets to know the family members and learns to meet their specific needs. In a staffed position the Nanny must also learn quickly to ascertain the nuances of politics and etiquette within a home:

What are the politics of the household?

- ☆ Who is in charge?

- ☆ Who has which responsibility and which authority?

- ☆ What is the service culture?

- ☆ What traditions of the household need to be supported?

- ☆ Who is the supervisor of the Nanny?

- ☆ To whom does the Nanny speak when she perceives that there is a problem or when the position is not working for the Nanny?

What is the etiquette of the household?

- ☆ Who is to answer the phone and door, and how?

- ☆ How do staff members enter a room when someone else is present?

- ☆ What do you do when your employer enters the room?

- ☆ How do you behave during family disputes?

☆ Who turns down the children's beds?

☆ How are children to dress for the day's events or when guests are present?

☆ Do the parents attend and/or announce special achievements of the children?

☆ How do you address your employers? Do you use their formal names?

☆ How/when do you communicate with the other members of the household staff?

☆ How/when do you communicate with your employer?

☆ Are there regularly scheduled meeting times?

☆ With whom are you able to speak freely?

☆ How do you handle gossip and privacy issues?

☆ What is the expected dress and behavior of the Nanny and the children during entertaining events?

☆ What are the standards for table manners and formal service etiquette?

☆ How does the Nanny position change when the Nanny and children are traveling with the parents?

In learning about the Nanny Management System, Nannies should keep in mind the following:

☆ Understand the values, priorities, and methods the parents choose for raising their children, and stick to them.

☆ Understand the concept of professional employment and make sure you're providing value in exchange for an appropriate salary.

☆ In addition to the actual childcare, be part of the overall work of the household, so that you might have an impact on the overall atmosphere and be a role model for your family's children. This will make a real difference in how other staff persons perceive you as well.

REASONS FOR CONFLICT BETWEEN NANNIES AND PARENTS

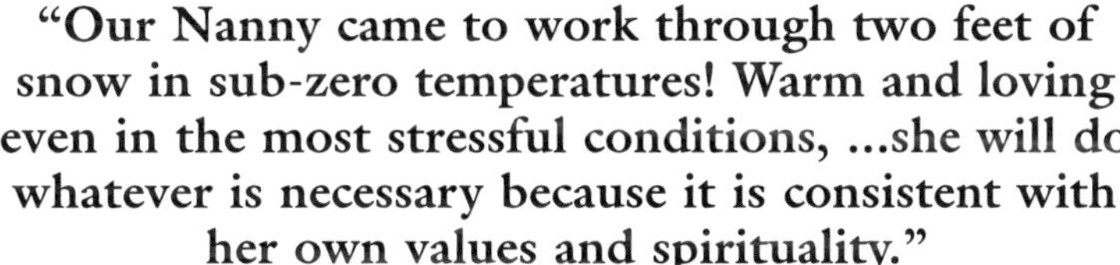

"Our Nanny came to work through two feet of snow in sub-zero temperatures! Warm and loving even in the most stressful conditions, ...she will do whatever is necessary because it is consistent with her own values and spirituality."

Starkey International has over time kept track of what works and does not work in the Nanny Industry. The following is a list of the most often cited or implied reasons for conflict.

No 'Starkey Style' written employment agreement
Lack of professional boundaries and mutual respect
Failure to understand the difference between 'stated' priorities and 'real' priorities

Failure to set up a service structure and Nanny Manager plan:
    Communicate Service Standards
    Set up and monitor Day in the Life Schedules
    Clearly communicate expectations

Lack of educational training
Lack of safety planning and precautions
Failure to keep confidentiality
Failure to understand and follow employer's parenting philosophy
Lack of good health and energy
Sloppiness/ poor personal appearance and personal habits
Lack of professionalism and ethical standards
Jealousy between parent and the Nanny
Differences in styles of discipline
Parent's failure to remain the "real parent"
Lack of planning for turnover/departure of Nanny and children experiencing loss
Nannies on-call twenty-four hours while family on vacation or traveling
Parental fear and suspicion of child abuse
Low salaries, benefits, and the failure to follow state and federal employment practices
Inability for Nannies to have personal life, limited privacy, scheduled time for other interests
Poor communication and destructive management styles

SUCCESSFUL CONDITIONS FOR NANNIES AND PARENTS

When the following have been achieved, the employer/Nanny relationship is generally successful. As in any relationship, no family or Nanny situation will be perfect. However, when using the following as a checklist of standards to work towards, chances are you will succeed.

☆ The appropriate Nanny is hired, possessing the right background and qualifications for the level of responsibility and age of children.

☆ Family standards and favorites have been identified and the Nanny holds these priorities in high regard.

☆ A service delivery system is established and is consistent with family standards and methods.

☆ The Nanny sets up Day in the Life schedules that communicate the manner and frequency of the children's overall physical care, emotional care, educational needs and social engagements.

☆ Schedules are created prior to the upcoming week and submitted to parents for their reference and approval.

☆ Relationship between parents and Nanny is mutually supportive and positive.

☆ The Nanny is managed fairly, with opportunity for success, criticized professionally, not personally, and supervised by only one person.

☆ The Nanny and the Nanny role are respected and supported within the home.

☆ The Nanny is emotionally and physically available to the family's children while actively on the job.

☆ The Nanny is able to teach and influence the children in a fashion consistent with the family's style of parenting — the family's agenda and not their own.

☆ The Nanny engages children in activities in a fashion consistent with the parents' philosophy.

☆ The Nanny understands the parenting philosophy about money, responsibilities, commitments, and the items about which the children may make choices on their own.

☆ The Nanny acts as a professional.

☆ The Nanny respects family decisions and clearly supports the parents' positions as the primary decision makers. The Nanny assumes decision-making responsibility only on issues clearly delegated.

☆ The Nanny demonstrates common sense and keeps the safety and welfare of the children as the utmost concern.

☆ The Nanny provides nutritional, well-balanced meals and snacks that meet with the children's needs.

☆ The Nanny schedules, monitors and supports any transportation/car-pool activities that are needed.

☆ The Nanny is provided with privacy, separate housing, separate entrance, or an over the garage apartment.

☆ The Nanny is supported in efforts to develop a private life, friends and educational pursuits away from the home.

☆ The personal problems, personal relationships, money problems, sex, religion and other individual rights are not discussed or judged.

☆ The Nanny is provided monetary compensation and benefits appropriate with a level of maturity, responsibility expected, education, and experience.

Confidentiality

Nannies in a private household must recognize that safeguarding the privacy of the employer, all communications and family life is the very foundation of this industry. Employers must be able to employ household support staff secure in the knowledge that the privacy of their home and family confidentiality will be kept at all times.

DEFINING THE RELATIONSHIP OF SERVICE

Personal Service as a professional industry in the United States is in its early growing stages. Individual consciousness and mutual communication are essential to success. Those going into personal service in the last quarter of the twentieth century, including Nannies, are the pioneers and entrepreneurs of this service. Starkey and The Starkey Nanny Management System are helping to position Nannying and other personal service careers as high-end career opportunities by establishing a new definition for the term *service*. This definition transcends an old service teaching premise that suggests "the customer is always right." In truth, those of us in service know that the employers are not always right, and that they can be demanding and unrealistic. By the same token, the service provider can be untrained, does not understand a service role, lacks appropriate service professionalism, and technical abilities. Furthermore, if this "customer is always right" premise is the service basis of both the person being served and the person serving, it generally assumes expectations that are both undefined and undeliverable. Ultimately, this "one side is always right" relationship promotes burnout, disinterest, and poor self-esteem on the part of the service provider and "you just can't find good service help" attitudes on the part of employers!

A dictionary associates the term "service" with the following occupations: servant, minister or priest, public servant or government employee, armed forces soldier and surprisingly, prostitute. Starkey anticipates that new meanings and public understanding will emerge as the relationship between individuals serving and those receiving the service is experienced. Service is a relationship and an art form, and highly personal for those directly involved.

PERSONAL SERVICE STATEMENT

Where Nannies are going in their service careers depends ultimately upon what is important to them. As Nannies experience and define their own individual **Service Standards**, priorities and life values, they will better understand those of their employers. Most Nannies are not able to perform a level of service in childcare that has not been trained or learned in a prior experience. Standards of "Nanny Service" are learned skills and can be seen by those around them. Personal Service Styles include:

☆ How one looks	☆ One's personal discipline
☆ How one speaks	☆ One's mindfulness
☆ How one handles oneself	☆ What one is good at
☆ What one says	☆ What one most enjoys doing
☆ How one anticipates needs	☆ How one defines quality of life

Within the Starkey training, students are expected to articulate their own **Personal Service Statement**. Personal Service Statements reflect a style or goals, not just unrelated activities. When parents begin to set up professional childcare within their home, parents and Nannies must work together to create or manifest the service standards of the household, while demonstrating the Nanny's own personal style of service. It is not realistic to expect otherwise. However, these two systems of thought must be cohesive. For most Nannies, it would be a new thought process to be conscious and mindful of their own individual service styles as well as the employer's Service Standards. They must be sure they are compatible, as every day the Nanny is helping create the life of the employer's children. *Service is one of the highest forms of relationship!*

A NOTE FOR THE NANNY:
As you think, so you will create!

Too often employment as a Nanny is seen as something for only young women to perform until something more "professional" is attained. This could not be farther from the truth. You must know that childcare is right for you, as a profession. Take a moment to listen to what your mind is saying.

☆ What are your thoughts about Nannying?

☆ Are your thoughts positive?

☆ Are you happy?

The process of creation has two steps to it, first the thinking process, then the manifestation or physical response to that thinking.

☆ What are your values, standards, morals and ethics?

☆ What do you really want to be?

☆ What do you want to do?

☆ What is it that you want to achieve right now in your life?

☆ Do you really want to be in service?

STARKEY'S DEFINITION OF SERVICE

Starkey states that service is possible only when the following ingredients are present. Service is defined as an alchemy of:

- ☆ a genuine relationship
- ☆ superior technical skills
- ☆ Master the Moment authority
- ☆ need to earn a living — self-motivation
- ☆ doing what you love to do

What is a genuine relationship in service?

It is a relationship whereby the persons giving and receiving are psychologically open and willing to be in the service experience. There cannot be any negativity in the way. As in all relationships, it takes active communication and work to create and maintain the relationship.

What are the superior technical skills of service?

The service provider must have technical skills which generally include childcare, management and people skills, organization, daily graces, some cleaning as it pertains to the children, household cooking, care of children's clothing, a high level of consciousness, and a resourceful nature.

What is Master the Moment authority of service?

This requires that the person delivering the service has not only the responsibility but the authority to deliver the service. This authority must extend itself so that new decisions can be made in a moment of crisis or change. It requires some management level decision making and appropriate authority to the demands of the position.

What is self-motivation in service?

It is a desire to find the answer or resource, to go beyond the call to create just the right feeling, along with having the self-discipline to complete the job when others have gone home, demanding a personal commitment and standards of excellence.

What is doing what you love to do in service?

Service is a way of life. It is a personal path in knowing that you are a service provider. One often knows they are a service provider early in life and only has difficulty finding a way to deliver their service.

Choosing Service

In the United States, there is a work ethic that has evolved over the last two centuries. It came from certain cultural and religious influences in early America. It was believed that to be "good" one had to work from sunrise to sunset and beyond, to be better than and to work harder than others, and to sacrifice present for future goals. One who did not live this way was not "good" and did not want to "get ahead." From this ideal of hard work to support the family and attain heaven has evolved the technological treadmill Americans often find themselves on. Our expectations for service also evolve from this perception. Clarifying what service is to you, both the parent and the Nanny, will enable a genuine service relationship to be achieved.

The Starkey Nanny Management System provides a complete view, from an administrative management perspective, of what is being requested of a Nanny. Those Nannies with service hearts by nature often forget to create, provide for and participate in their own lives, separate from their employers. This very quickly causes a service heart to harden and burn out. A cup of nourishment that is emptied has nothing to give. Service that is superior is provided by service professionals who are balanced and well-fed themselves.

THE STARKEY NANNY MANAGEMENT SYSTEM

INTRODUCTION

Mrs. Starkey's Nanny Management System evolved from the better part of two decades of working in and placing household staff and Nannies in private homes, and observing what made a successful household service relationship. Excerpts have been taken from Starkey's Household Management System, currently utilized for teaching the management of large and sophisticated homes. It is not patterned after the British servant heritage nor the slave servants in American history. As this method of management is applied in a home that employs a Nanny, it educates the Nanny about the specific needs of the family and the household. The system is interactive and is an information and communication process that both educates and organizes. It provides perspective for both the employer and the Nanny.

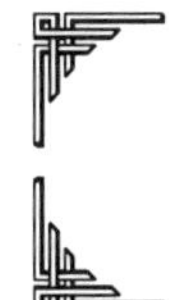 

The Starkey Nanny Management System organizes the Nanny service delivery structure.

This educational process adapts to any family, for any level of household, and identifies specific Service Standards, the environment, household priorities, family favorites, and individual life styles. It ultimately organizes daily working schedules; **Day in the Life**, **Daily**

Graces and cleaning; play time and meal time; and it also delineates expectations. It gives the employer and the Nanny an understanding of the daily challenges. It also upgrades the persona and self-image of the Nanny.

The Starkey Nanny Management System introduces a new set of terms to bring attention to concepts and a process that must be understood by both the employer and the Nanny. Those terms are: **The Starkey Relationship of Service**, **Service Standards**, **The Environment**, **Personal and Household Favorites**, **Day in the Life**, **Household Standards**, and the **Nanny Manager's Book**. These terms are also defined in Appendix A in this book.

> **The Starkey Nanny Management System is a process that manages service expectations.**

It is not an easy process but is considered *professionalism* in personal service. It requires a service relationship between the Nanny and the principals of the family. They must be willing to communicate on a regular basis. It requires trust on the part of the family and it requires self-esteem, technical knowledge, organization, professionalism and wisdom on the part of the Nanny. It is not a quick process. It requires planning, directed time and thoughtful consideration. It can often take up to three months to work through the transitional process and set up the Nanny Manager System. After all, this is an ongoing relationship and will not be created in one day!

OVERVIEW OF THE STARKEY NANNY MANAGEMENT SYSTEM

The process begins by first identifying the household **Environment,** that is to say, the physical home, the property, where it is located, who the family members are and their family history. Once the environment is defined, one can then begin to set up the administrative plan for the overall service delivery and the care of the children.

The **Nanny Management System** next identifies the family's **Personal Standards** and **Favorites.** Family goals and values, household, parent and children's priorities, the employer's general daily schedule and examples of the children's daily schedules are learned here. This will also include the **Daily Graces** to be performed by the Nanny. Daily Graces are the tasks that are done daily to open or close a home and to bring it back to a state of order.

The next task is to identify Service Standards within the home. Service Standards organize all of the favorites and household standards within a home. These standards may include: administrative duties and cleaning that must be performed in regard to the children, a cooking style and favorite children's menus, clothing favorites and clothing care, entertaining styles, the need for security and safety issues, transportation and schedules, and finally, the children's education and care.

From all of this information, the actual weekly **Day in the Life** or the daily duties and schedules for the children and the Nanny are developed.

This information is placed in a clear organizational system called **The Nanny Manager Book**. This book provides for the daily log of the Nanny's and children's schedules, reminders of the last time toys were sanitized, favorite books, examples of favorite menus, when the last booster shots were given, special friends' birthdays, and more. It organizes your Nanny and your childcare service delivery.

*The forms to complete the Nanny Management System and create your own **Nanny Manager's Book** can be ordered by contacting Starkey International's corporate office.*

The Environment and the Family Tree
Physical location
The size of the home and property
Demographics — who are they, who lives at home
Traditions, Values, Medical histories
Education, Religion, Philosophy

Personal Standards and Household Favorites
Personal/household favorites
Children's favorites
Employer's and children's schedules
Styles of communication

Service Standards and Nanny Management
Administrative Standards What and when are the daily/weekly schedules, play dates for the children? Doctors' appointments?
Cleaning Standards/Daily Graces What are the daily graces in your household and the time you do them?
Maintenance Standards Who safety proofs the home and how often is it checked?
Grounds and Property Standards Where are children allowed outside, is there a pool, are there terrain hazards?
Valet/Clothing Standards When do you launder and iron children's clothing or organize closets?
Cooking Standards When are meal times at your household? Who prepares the meals?
Entertaining Standards What kinds of parties do the children attend?
Transportation and Travel Standards When do you drive the children to activities?
Security Standards What are the special concerns regarding the safety and security of your children?
Child Education/Care Standards What are the play times at your household, crafts and favorite activities?

Day in The Life of the Nanny
What is the household structure: the number of service staff working in the home?
Does the Nanny's Day in the Life support the family's schedules?
When is your Nanny's start time and ending time?
When are morning and evening Graces?
When do you communicate with your employers?
When are children's outdoor times?
When does your Nanny have her meals? When does the family have their meals?
When do the children nap?
What time do the children spend with their parents?
What time do the children go to sleep at night?

THE ENVIRONMENT AND THE FAMILY TREE

Surrounding this **Relationship of Service** is what we call the **Environment and the Family Tree**. All service delivery to children and to their family takes place in a specific home or homes, in a certain social and geographical space.

This Environment can have an enormous impact on the people who provide service, determining how it is provided, the difficulty factor in providing the service and what service actually takes place.

The concept of the Environment encompasses both the actual place in which the service occurs and the individual people for whom the service is being provided.

Family Tree information will include family traditions, medical histories, religious or cultural customs, educational expectations, family home histories, and family businesses.

The table on the following page outlines some questions that generally need to be answered to begin the process of the **Starkey Nanny Management System**. The table identifies the physical location, the physical house, the people, other additional aspects that need care, the household expenses, and finally, how you begin to analyze what you now know.

This information about the household and the surrounding area is essential prior to identifying the service standards and specific needs within each home.

THE ENVIRONMENT AND THE FAMILY TREE
Examples

Item	Details	Examples
Physical location	Climate, Urban Access, Rural, Neighborhood, surrounding areas	Weather, hurricane, floods, earthquakes, amount of precipitation, seasons, near a city, school and shopping proximity, house style, residential, rural or commercial area, coastline, water proximity, mountains, desert
House	Structure, age, size, security needs, safety issues with children and energy resources	Style, condition, square footage, property size, number of acres, intrusion alarms, security gates, bodyguards
People	Family, single/married/ number of children, parent relationships with each other, extended families, former marriages, number of guests that visit, nationality, religion, personalities, current household staff, contract vendors	Who is in the house, age of children, lifestyles, background, age of parents, service perceptions, medical health, habits, ethics, relationships, expectations, play/education, parents' experience with Nannies, and parent attitudes, security and public personalities
Other	Vehicles, pets, gardens, valuables and collectibles, formality of household	Household cars, vans, recreational/sports equipment, dogs, cats, livestock, horses, flower or vegetable gardens, orchards, pools, tennis courts, yacht, plane, antiques, vintage cars, art collections, where smoking is permitted
Expenses	Children's expenses, Nanny's budget, food, security, entertainment, travel	Weekly/monthly budget, petty cash fund
Analysis	Based on where the home is, the size of property, who lives there, the number of children, their personalities, their frame of reference regarding service and their lifestyle, what style or kind of service, what are the personalities of the children, what are the hours of the staff, what Nanny coverage is being requested	The family household priorities, expected management style, level and kind of child management required in the household, the service style and kind of Nanny and support staff required to carry out the childcare request, live-in or -out position, type of housing provided, salary and benefits

PERSONAL STANDARDS AND HOUSEHOLD FAVORITES

In the first week everyone will be gathering a great deal of information. The parents will begin talking about the things they like and what they want for their children. A Nanny's first days will require intense observation of every aspect of the position and the family. The Nanny and the employer will also require several planned communication meetings. Personal Styles or Favorites are unique to each household and often to each individual. Examples of the kinds of questions Nannies might ask, and the information parents need to provide, follow in the section titled, "Implementing the Starkey Nanny Management System."

The Nanny's ability to analyze family priorities and the daily patterns of the parents and the children and to be resourceful in obtaining answers is part of the art form in the service industry. Many families who are new to household service have never considered that this information is needed. The Nanny often is overwhelmed at having to guess the answers to perform her job. None of us do well or appreciate having to work in a crisis mode. The Nanny often guesses wrong and ultimately feels demoralized and incapable in the process. Nannying is very difficult until the rules of the home become clear. Household favorites or parent favorites may be quite different from each child's individual favorites and the Nanny should be advised as to whose favorites take precedence at different times and places.

Employers must inform their Nannies about their children and about each child's specific needs and likes. Knowing these details puts the Nanny in a position to organize each day's activities, carry out the desires of the parents and deliver a superior level of personal childcare service. Regular, structured weekly communication meetings should be set up between the parents and the Nanny immediately.

It is fundamental within the American culture to be proud of and to defend individuality.

Please remember, Starkey does not judge nor recommend particular service standards, preferences, or styles of service. It is only important that each family recognize that they do indeed have standards, and that to obtain a quality service, these standards must be defined.

SERVICE STANDARDS AND NANNY MANAGEMENT

The higher the structure, the higher the service delivery.

The ultimate *goal* for the Nanny is to understand, manage and carry out the Service Standards in any household. **The process of learning the Service Standards of the employer puts into play a "service delivery structure" and the Starkey System of Nanny Management.**

What are Service Standards and how does one learn what another's service standard might be?

We use the term Service Standards
to define the level of service being requested within the environment. It mirrors and supports the environment and its inhabitants. It is the physical, the unique individuality and the personality that are seen and experienced by the children, the children's parents and extended family and other guests entering the home. Service Standards are developed and set by the parent and they reflect the family's priorities, personal idiosyncrasies, lifestyle, daily schedules, personal needs, favorites, and relationships within that home. The absence of service standards can also be easily recognized and experienced.

The Starkey System of Nanny Management
sets up the service delivery system to provide those precise service standards for the children and those visiting the home. Exact service standards are learned by identifying the specific favorites of each family member and the household.

The Starkey System
requires that each standard category: The Administrative, Cleaning, Maintenance, Grounds and Property, Clothing, Cooking, Entertaining, Security, Transportation and Travel, and Child Education/Care be discussed thoroughly to identify the specific service standards and favorites of the household and be placed into the overall service plan. This is the next step in the process of developing the overall service delivery system. Each area is systematically organized with the necessary service definitions, how to's, household and personal styles and favorites, and administrative schedules to support the service standard.

This is where most Nannies have difficulty. To the inexperienced, Nannying is thought to be strictly childcare, some cooking and cleaning, and how well it is done. It is necessary to have most if not all of these technical skills when beginning a position. However, it is the relationship between the Nanny, the parent and the children, and the Nanny's ability to plan and perform duties at the level and in the specific style that the household requests that makes a successful career path.

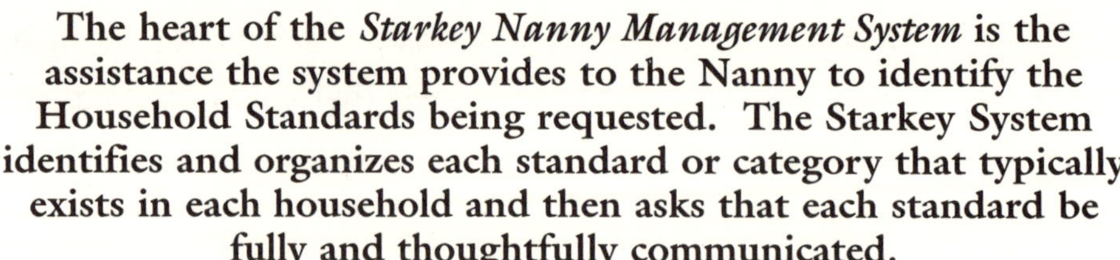

The heart of the *Starkey Nanny Management System* is the assistance the system provides to the Nanny to identify the Household Standards being requested. The Starkey System identifies and organizes each standard or category that typically exists in each household and then asks that each standard be fully and thoughtfully communicated.

Today, most parent employers do not know what they are asking for or how to get it, so the Nanny arrives at a position and begins performing childcare and household duties as they come up, and performs them as they personally have always done.

It is much easier to see the family next door, how they live, their style of food, how well their children are taken care of than it is to see ourselves. We often do not realize what it is we do or what we want until one day we awaken to find that our way of taking care of the children has disappeared. We then attempt to discover the cause. Typically, it is the Nanny who has just spent the last six months setting up a standard of childcare and lifestyle that is foreign to us. It is at this point that parents ask their Nanny, "Whose agenda are you on, yours or mine?"

Some tasks are done daily in a household. The frequency of their occurrence lends structure to a home and requires that they be done with a special grace. Starkey refers to these duties as **Daily Graces**. Specifically, these duties are generally not the heavy cleaning required in a home, but those done each morning and again in the evening.

> Morning Graces include: opening the home by raising blinds or opening the curtains, turning off the security system, walking through the children's areas so that the Nanny will learn what occurred the night before. The Nanny will pick up glasses, snack plates, clean toys, and put clothing back into their right places. Depending upon whether or not there is a Household Manager in the home, the Nanny might also put pillows back in place, observe light cleaning needs, answer the door, occasionally supervise vendors, replace burned-out light bulbs, pluck dead leaves on plants and generally bring the house back into a state of order. In some households

the Nanny might also be responsible for making beds, freshening bathrooms, unloading the dishwasher and cleaning up the breakfast dishes. Evening Graces include the reverse: closing the home, checking and closing windows and curtains, turning on the security system, turning the lights on, straightening the household from the children's daytime activities, turning down beds, and cleaning up after dinner.

Once the **Personal Standards**, the **Favorites,** the **Daily Graces** and the **Service Standards** are identified, they should be maintained and carried out. These standards are communicated by the employers, and maintained through the Nanny's ability to plan, and communicate to the children and others associated with the children. The Nanny must provide for children "the employer's way." It is through this communication and training that the Nanny's experience and professionalism will sustain the standards and upgrade the parents' and the children's quality of life.

OVERVIEW OF HOUSEHOLD SERVICE STANDARDS

Once the concepts surrounding the environment and the favorites are understood, household service standards must be identified and placed into perspective. The process of identification begins with each of the household service standard categories indicated below. In each category the service standard is identified, household style or favorites are identified, and the methods or organizational structure for upholding the standard begins to take place. The information shown in the table below is one example.

Category	Service Standard	Styles/favorites	Examples/tasks
Administrative Management	Professional and relationship oriented.	Busy, Type A personality monthly accounting of expense reports, kind, asks lots of questions, wants their children to have the best. Generous!	Computer, Day in the Life records, Nanny Management book, Nanny expense account, and petty cash.
Daily Graces and Cleaning	Sanitized, organized and a place for everything and everything in its place. Family comfortable clean! Prefers environmentally safe products and likes clean smell, seven-day coverage.	One child allergic to dust, likes lemon fragrances, morning clean-up by 10:00 am, detailed, careful style. Two inside cats.	Make children's beds, pick up toys, sanitize children's bathrooms, sanitize children's toys. Bedrooms, living room and playrooms vacuumed while children out of the house 2x per week. Clean up after meals.
Grounds and Property	300 acres of land, wooded area, and cliffs, on lake, pool area.	Toddler and pre-school children. Children's playground, two outside dogs.	Gates to pool area locked, children always supervised when outside, children taught to swim at very early age etc., taught to respect animals.
Cooking	Fresh daily, organic, filtered water, immaculate kitchen, environmental doors to hold smells, nutritious, no junk food, no sugar after 5:00 pm.	Family does not eat red meat, prefers fish, chicken and pork grilled, no cream sauces, spinach salads, fresh breads and muffins, southern desserts available on the weekends. Plated service or family style. Family eats primarily in breakfast room.	Developed menus specially for children recognizing family favorites and comfort foods, stock refrigerators with healthy snacks in each zone, manners and table settings for each meal, daily grocery shopping. Nanny prepares breakfast, lunch. Dinner is prepared by household chef.

Category	Service Standard	Styles/favorites	Examples/tasks
Entertaining	Separate catering kitchen for large parties, family entertains weekly, public personalities, statesmen, international protocol, formal table and service, personal friendly style, anything over 12 persons is catered. Children's parties monthly.	Grilled lamb, new potatoes and chocolate pie family favorite, Christian holidays always observed with family dinner, plated or Russian service used. Children's birthdays celebrated with large parties.	Prefers Nanny to coordinate everything regarding children's participation. Develop entertaining, "Ballet of Service styles" for each kind of children's event. Children always well dressed.
Maintenance	State of the art "Smart House", automatic lighting, environmental air conditioning unit.	One child just crawling, several story home, many steps, and fine antiques, hardwood floors.	Safety latches on doors, cupboards, gates in front of stairs, sharp edges with antique furniture, wood floors need polyurethane.
Security	Family very private and security conscious. Security system in homes. Hired security shared by four brothers, separate families. Several residences. Large family fortune, new money, never encountered a problem, located in small Midwestern city.	Family prefers to attend church alone, children picked up after school, spend summers at the lake. Mrs. does not like children to ever be without family or Nanny present.	Security team of 10 always in place for properties and the family. Coordinate daily schedules, attentive to security with children, children never left alone, security checks and family privacy always protected.
Transportation and Travel	Family cars typically include foreign high-end. Travel is international and domestic and always first class. Family owns travel agency, high-end hotels, chauffeured town car at home, corporate jet often utilized by family. 150 ft yacht anchored in Bahamas.	Prefers fun last-minute adventures, likes warm weather, likes pro tennis matches, likes the St. Regis or the Four Seasons, prefers to have family outings alone occasionally, security to provide driving.	All children's schedules must be communicated and coordinated with security staff. They typically also drive for the family. Attention to transportation needs of the children. Cars detailed and washed weekly by security staff. Heavy security requirements, children never left unsupervised when traveling.

Category	Service Standard	Styles/favorites	Examples/tasks
Clothing Care	Kids clean polished look, clothes high-end, designer level children's. Children's clothes all pressed. State of the art closets.	Gap, Gymboree, pinks and greens for the girls, Mouse Feathers, Flap Doodles, Heart Strings, Ocean Pacific, London Fog, Rothschild coats.	Dry cleaning and clothing inventory, personal shopper at Nordstrom and specialty shops, washing, pressing and mending at home. Jiffy steamer in each closet, sheets changed 2x per week or as needed. Dry cleaner picks up 2x per week.
Child Education/ Care	Traditional values, kind, and fair. Learn the value of earning one's way, do not tolerate laziness or over indulgence, values education and Republican philosophy, children's friends always welcome, family traditions support-ed, etiquette and manners always expected.	Weekly family outings, discipline is handled with communication and withdrawal of privileges. Catholic religion, attend Mass on Sundays as a family, enrolled in private schools, thinking about home schooling and educational goals.	Nannies scheduled seven days per week, pro-fessionally trained. Child-ren's friends treated with respect, cookies or snacks available. Sunday formal dinners prepared, family values supported. Daily alphabet practice. Arts and crafts.

DAY IN THE LIFE OF THE NANNY

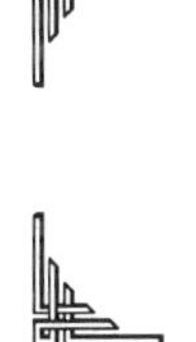

The *Day in the Life* is the power within the service delivery system. It is the place where the Nanny Manager "earns their keep" and is able to display the management form of Nanny service.

The final ongoing piece of the Starkey System of Nanny Management is the Day in the Life. This phrase is what Starkey uses to describe the daily household schedules and to report the everyday activities of the Nanny, the children and even the employers. This process implements the Nanny Management System in the daily duties of the Nanny. It showcases the Service Standards, Favorites, and priorities of the parents, manages the children's and the Nanny's time, and ultimately communicates to the parent what takes place every day within the home.

The Day in the Life is designed to be completely interactive between the Nanny and the employer. It provides the employer the opportunity to fine tune their Nanny service delivery system. As it comes into place, the Day in the Life trains and directs the entire household as it relates to the children.

It takes considerable time and energy to create a home and a child's atmosphere. Nannies are not often required to create the written plan, present it to the parents for approval and then put it into place. However, the Nanny Management System in many cases will be introducing a whole new quality of life to the children. Using the Day in the Life, the experience of order, warmth, creativity and safety is more than possible. The Nanny will contribute to the resurrection of the "mother at home" in America.

Throughout the early stages of obtaining information, the Nanny's ultimate goal is to create the Day in the Life. The task of creating the Day in the Life will develop a system for organizational structure and daily schedules for children and the Nanny in the household. Upon arriving at a new position, and depending upon experience and expertise, the Nanny will create Day in the Life schedules for some or all of the duties listed on page 56.

The Nanny in performing each duty, will learn how long each task takes and how often they must be done.

- ☆ Provide childcare
- ☆ Observe and participate in the daily schedule of the children
- ☆ Identify and provide for the Nanny Daily Graces
- ☆ Baby proof and make safe the home and other areas the children visit
- ☆ Care for the emotional and nurturing needs of the children
- ☆ Purchase food, toys, safety items and other children's needs such as clothing and furniture
- ☆ Create games, crafts, music and other educational activities that challenge and direct children
- ☆ Plan suitable menus and support healthy eating habits
- ☆ Be responsible for the preparation, presentation and service of foods and snacks
- ☆ Care for the children's closets, launder, press, and steam clothing, and polish shoes
- ☆ Prepare travel arrangements, pack and unpack clothing
- ☆ Arrange car seats, buckle seat belts, and drive for the children
- ☆ Arrange for welcome and care for children's playmates and guests in the home
- ☆ Plan the children's entertaining events
- ☆ Arrange and supervise birthday and holiday parties
- ☆ Supervise and train any Nanny part-time support
- ☆ Answer the telephone and door, take and relay messages
- ☆ Supervise any household vendors

*Use The Household Manager's Software to list
these weekly tasks quickly and efficiently.*

It is impossible to do it all or have it all done at once. Most household Nannies arrive at a new position and begin responding to the immediate needs of the home. We call this being reactive. In most time management circles it is called working in a crisis mode. Time management experts counsel that if one spends more time planning, one will be able to perform in a pro-active mode and will have a much better opportunity to accomplish goals.

The Nanny will be maintaining the standards that have been set by the employer, by establishing the daily routine, including daily graces, organizing the overall childcare plan, hiring the additional help needed, and by example, training and supervising support vendors and the other support staff in the household.

It is ultimately the Nanny's responsibility to keep the children directed, cared for, nurtured and well-fed. But it may also be the Nanny's responsibility to keep the children's bathrooms polished and sanitized, the child's playroom orderly, the kitchen spotless and organized, the children's laundry done, and be available to the employer for extra projects or errands, see that the children have play dates with friends, and prepare dinner, etc.

Each household has different priorities, time tables, and needs.

The Day in the Life schedules provide in written organizational terms what is actually being requested. Day in the Life schedules must be organized for each day of each week. They determine, in advance, what and when tasks need to be done, for each child, for each task. They define every task for each of the Service Standards, how long each task will take, and how often to accomplish each task, even what room or product to use in each case.

Day in the Life schedules organize all tasks effectively within a given period of time, so that if Grandmother Jennie makes an unexpected visit from Florida to see her grandchildren, or the special play friend appears at the door, both the parent and the Nanny know what might not be accomplished that day. The Nanny can master the moment by welcoming the visitors in the home, helping them to unpack in the guest quarters, and quickly rearranging a planned meal.

The Day in the Life also supports the employer and the Nanny to decide together, if needed, when a specific task should be completed, rescheduled or canceled altogether! Remember, Day in the Life schedules must be completed weekly to be effective.

The critical theme for any household is to create a pattern or system and make it routine. Children love being able to depend upon things to happen. Certain tasks have to be completed every day to keep things at the standard that everyone enjoys.

The opening and closing of the house, daily graces, and the rest of the daily routine in each home is unique to each household. In some households, routines are already established. For instance, Monday is planning day, every Tuesday might be laundry day, every Wednesday is play date day and the outside shopping is accomplished, or every Thursday we bake something special and it is the day the sheets are changed on the beds. Every Friday the organization is accomplished for the family's weekend.

In these cases, the Day in the Life schedule indicates what needs to be accomplished before the physical evidence does. It is essential for the Nanny to follow the schedule and to create a routine rather than trying to remember things.

With schedule changes, days off, continual household activity, house guests, entertaining events and children's car pooling and school schedules, you have better things to do with the available space in your brain than to remember what is to be done with Daily Graces, grocery shopping, or laundry schedule on a particular day. Examples of Day in the Life schedules can be found in the following section.

☆ 59 ☆

IMPLEMENTING THE STARKEY NANNY MANAGEMENT SYSTEM

On the following pages are examples of questions developed by Starkey International to walk the employer and the Nanny through the **Starkey Nanny Management System**. We have provided many possible questions and answers as a reference so that the reader might fully understand the nature of the information required in order to serve a family. It is understood that this information is asked only as appropriate and necessary for the situation.

The goal for the Nanny is to understand the family, to take on the professional's role, and to care for the children. The goal for the parents is to fully understand the nature of their own lifestyle and what they are asking a Nanny to accomplish.

For the following Starkey Nanny Management System sample, we have chosen a single father who shares the custody of two children with his former wife. This demonstrates how he and his Nanny implement the Starkey System for him, his children, his extended family and individual needs. His former wife also has a Nanny. We have included information about the children's mother and grandparents so that the Nanny is made fully aware and able to support the children's complete family system. We have chosen this example as it best exemplifies how multi-dimensional our individual lifestyles really are.

Family and Family Tree	
Names of people in family and ages?	*Anders Hoyle, age 38* *Meredith , age 4* *Valerie, age 2* *Ex-wife, Elizabeth Hoyle Templeton, age 38*
Household pets? Are they inside or outside?	*Frumby the adopted cat, long hair and white, inside only* *Gerble the Gerbil, inside cage only* *Fernando the fish, inside bowl only* *Mother has shar-pei, Leroy, who stays outdoors during the day.*
Who else lives in the home?	*Mr. Anders Hoyle, Sr., age 67. International photographer who travels extensively, but maintains a visitor's room in the home.*
Family Tree and Adult Family Background. Traditions and Medical histories Parents Grandparents Great-Grandparents	***Family Name:*** *Hoyle* ***Father:*** *Anders Hoyle, age 38, born and raised in Lake Forest, Illinois. Started photography business in 1983 while at Harvard Business School. Works out regularly, watches his cholesterol due to family history of heart attack.* ***Mother:*** *Elizabeth Rohl Hoyle Templeton, age 38, food allergies, born and raised Bellevue, Washington, former model, married Anders in 1984 and divorced in 1996. Married John Templeton in 1997. Took home two blocks from Anders' family home to co-parent children.* ***Paternal Grandparents:*** *Father Anders Hoyle, Sr., Mother Sara Erickson Hoyle (deceased) heart attack at age 50. Father international photographer, age 67, still very active and in good health. Both from Minneapolis, Minnesota, first generation in U.S. Both university educated.* ***Maternal Grandparents:*** *Father John Robert Rohl, age 65, high blood pressure, owns successful imported car dealerships in Seattle area. Mother, Martha Kenney Rohl, age 63, problems with food allergies, housewife, member of Junior League and known community volunteer.* ***Paternal Great-Grandfather:*** *Eric Roderick Hoyle (deceased), heart attack age 52. Great Grandmother, Eva Swensson Hoyle, age 92, still active in family life. Grande dame of clan, lives locally.* ***Maternal Great-Grandfather:*** *John Frederick Rohl, age 87, in frail health, due to high blood pressure and strokes. Great Grandmother Eleanor Bingley Rohl, age 86, in good health. Visits great grandchildren when husband can travel.*

Family and Family Tree	
Hometown - raised where?	Anders was raised in Lake Forest, in private schools, athlete in High School. Grew up in staffed household. Elizabeth was raised in Bellevue, attended local public schools until High School. Active in community service throughout childhood. Grew up in staffed household.
Schools attended: major field of study	Anders, Northwestern University, BA Photography; MBA from Harvard. Elizabeth, Marymount University, Chicago, BA Fine Arts.
Extended family involvement, family gatherings?	Family potluck dinners on Sundays, including grandparents, ex-wife and her family; birthdays, holidays very important. Great-grandparents attend when possible. Family very artistic, visit art museums together often, children supported in their artistic talents.
Style of parenting experienced during childhood?	Dr. Spock, children treated with respect, but expected to be responsible members of the family and community.
Family conflicts?	Extended family uncomfortable with divorce; trust issues, occasional conflicts with extended family over time with grandchildren. Occasional arguments over philosophical issues regarding religious beliefs or politics.
Patterns of family medical problems that are repeated?	Heart attack (paternal grandmother, great grandfather), high blood pressure and strokes (maternal side), food allergies (maternal side).
Pattern of family businesses that are repeated?	Photography, paternal side for 3 generations; Car dealerships, maternal side for 2 generations.
Family lifestyle patterns and rules that are repeated?	Parents treat children with respect, expected to be responsible, contributing members of the family and community.
Overall coverage requested including days and time?	Nanny, weekdays, 7:30 AM through 6:30 PM. Nanny helps with potluck dinner on Sunday afternoons.
Household sq. ft. and number of acres? Describe outside grounds.	5,000 sq. ft. Home; outside, 2 acres, with flower gardens, lawns, and children's garden, where children are learning to grow and care for vegetables.
Collectibles?	Father has extensive collection of Asian Art, including brush paintings and sculptures.

<table>
<tr><td colspan="2" align="center">Family Goals</td></tr>
<tr><td colspan="2" align="center">"Good Order is the Foundation of all Things"-Edmund Burke</td></tr>
<tr>
<td>What are the family goals?</td>
<td>1. Loving, stable family life
2. Making a difference
3. Love and support of extended family including former wife and in-laws</td>
</tr>
<tr>
<td>What is the employer's Philosophy of Service?</td>
<td>A conscious and genuine give and take, gracious and appreciative.</td>
</tr>
<tr>
<td>What are the three key issues the parents feel are most important with regard to the children?</td>
<td>1. Safety
2. Art and Education
3. Feeling loved</td>
</tr>
<tr>
<td>What has been the history with past Nannies and other household staff?</td>
<td>Dad and mother (former wife) have had several part-time babysitters, now Dad wants the care of a professional for his children.

All have continued to connect with the children over the years by being invited to birthday parties. One has moved to another city.</td>
</tr>
</table>

Family Values	
What type of service do you want in your home? Casual, formal or a combination?	*Anders likes casual style for leisure, but formal for entertaining.*
How often do you entertain and who do you entertain?	*Anders hosts monthly gatherings of his photography organization. Weekly extended family gatherings.*
List the importance of the following areas: career, community, family, spirituality.	*Career is important, but children's needs very important to both parents. Community service is next priority.*
Who makes the final decisions in the household if there is a difference of opinions?	*Anders is the authority for everything under his roof.*
How much time do you spend with the children in a week?	*Anders spends 3-5 hours during the week with the children; every other weekend, and Sunday afternoons.*
What type of activities do you participate in with the children?	*Museums of all types: Art, History, Natural History, Children's Museum, parks, bike rides (Anders pulls girls in toddler trailer).*
Who makes the final decisions concerning the child?	*Anders and Elizabeth confer with each other regarding joint decisions for children; otherwise, each decides in own home, as appropriate.*
What ethical values do you want the children to learn?	*Honesty, integrity, community service.*
What religious values do you want the children to learn?	*Anders and Elizabeth have agreed to have them follow religious instruction in both Lutheran and Catholic religions.*
What are the three most important things that you would like to see the children do on a daily basis?	*1. Pre-reading skills, fostering enjoyment of reading.* *2. Art project of any sort.* *3. Physical activity for at least 30 minutes.*
What do you see in the future for your child in regards to education?	*Children are expected to complete college.*
How often do you travel as a family?	*The children travel with Anders during his 3-week vacation to Europe every year.*

Family Values	
Does the Nanny travel with the family?	*Yes.*
Do you consider yourself pro-active or reactive about issues involving the children?	*Anders is definitely pro-active in all issues regarding his children.*
What does clean mean to you?	*To Anders, clean means clean "through and through": under items, behind them, etc.*
What does organized mean to you?	*"A place for everything, and everything in its place."*
What type of relationship do you want with your Nanny?	*Give and take, employer/employee, with mutual respect and support.*
What type of relationship do you want your Nanny to have with your children?	*Nurturing, "a teacher," loving, stable.*
Is security an issue for the house and the family?	*Not at this time.*
What do you want the Nanny to wear?	*Street clothes when out with children, khaki, denim dress or skirt when at home with children.*
What types of foods do you want the children to eat? Allergies?	*Anders is interested in high-protein, low-fat cooking for himself and the children, with occasional "treats." Ex-wife and children have food allergies, so those foods are avoided.*
What are children taught regarding table manners?	*Meredith is learning proper eating utensils and etiquette. Valerie is learning to use a fork and /or spoon properly.*
What are children taught regarding moral values?	*The children are being taught moral values consistent with the religious heritage of both families.*
What are children to be taught regarding environmental safety in and out of the house?	*The children have knowledge about safety regarding electrical wires, plugs; also learning water safety in their swimming lessons.*
What responsibilities are the children to have in keeping their area clean?	*The children are being taught to pick up after themselves, not to play with new items until former items are put away, to straighten their beds to age-appropriate standards, to put their laundry in the hamper.*

Personal Favorites — Family — General	
Marriages, first, second?	*Anders, divorced from first wife; Elizabeth, married to second husband.*
Religion?	*Anders, Lutheran background; Elizabeth, Catholic background.*
Extended family's religious beliefs if different from employer?	*Anders' family all Lutheran; Elizabeth's family all Catholic.*
Political beliefs?	*Hoyles are Democrats, Rohls are Republicans.*
Civic projects of special interest?	*The Fine Arts, and the Art Museum, Photography in the Schools Project.*
Memberships, Organizations?	*Fine Arts Guild, Junior League, Local Photography Association.*
Avocations and hobbies?	*Anders jogs 25 miles per week, participates in 10-K runs around the country; works out at health club on his lunch hour.*
Travel - How often, national and international?	*Dad travels quarterly for above-mentioned runs; monthly business travel to out-of state facilities.*
Style of decor - special colors?	*Likes Ralph Lauren, particularly Chaps.*
Style of dress, favorite clothes of parents?	*Business: suits; leisure: Ralph Lauren jeans, work shirt, boots.*
Time of day - am or pm parents?	*Morning person: awakens at 5, has morning run.*
Communication style, list maker.... talker.....want one person?	*Anders likes lists and organization.*
Leisure activities of parents?	*Active, outdoor activities. Fine Arts activities, civic activities.*
Cars owned, boats, other 'toys'?	*1971 Porsche 911, 1966 Mustang Convertible, 1997 Range Rover.*
Physical challenges, if any?	*Watching cholesterol in diet.*
Learning challenges, if any?	*None.*
Particular dislikes?	*Television, microwave cooking.*

Child's Favorites — Name: *Hoyle Children*	
"Specials" in child's life	Meredith: loves Nature walks, collecting rocks, sea shells. Valerie: loves being read to; "blankie."
Best friend(s)	Meredith's best friend is Mimi, a neighbor's child. Valerie does not yet have a best friend, calls Mother's shar-pei, Leroy, her best friend.
Favorite toy	Meredith: Elmo stuffed animal. Valerie: Velveteen Rabbit puppet.
Favorite blanket	Meredith: pink crochet baby blanket. Valerie: quilted blanket made by Great-Grandma Hoyle.
Favorite room	Meredith: her own room. Valerie: Meredith's room.
Favorite drink	Meredith: Cocoa, with whipped cream on top. Valerie: Chocolate milk.
Favorite food	Meredith: custard. Valerie: tapioca pudding.
Favorite book	Meredith: Curious George, and Madeline. Valerie: The Velveteen Rabbit.
Teachers, mentors, practitioners as concern the child and their activities	Nanny and Maria Norton, swimming instructor.

Parent's Schedule	Who: *Anders Hoyle*
Time	**Activities**
5:00am-6:00am Daily, except Mondays	Awakens and goes for morning run. On Mondays, Anders dresses at this hour.
6:00am-6:30am Daily	Showers and dresses for day.
6:30am-7:30am Daily	Awakens children, has breakfast with them.
7:30am-8:00am Daily	Leaves for work, commutes to office.
8:00am-12:30pm Daily	Morning meetings, activities.
12:30pm-1:30 pm Daily, except Mondays	Workout.
12:30pm-1:30pm Mondays	Weekly meeting with Nanny, by telephone, and alternately comes home for lunch and talks directly with Nanny.
1:30pm-5:30pm	Afternoon meetings, activities.
5:30pm-6:00pm	Commutes home.
6:00pm-7:00pm	Dinner with children.
7:00pm-8:30pm	Putting children to bed: Reading stories, quality time with them.
8:30pm-11:00pm	Personal time for work, reading, etc.

Child's Schedule	Who: *Hoyle Children*
Time	**Activities**
6:30am-7:30am Daily	*Awakened by Dad.* *Breakfast with Dad.*
7:30am-8:00am Daily	*Nanny helps children dress for day.*
8:00am-10:00am Daily	*Daily Graces: Reordering room with Nanny. Picking up toys, other items from around the house.*
10:00am-11:30am Daily	*Morning walk with Nanny, outside play, weather permitting. If not, reading, indoor play.*
11:30am-12 noon Daily	*Lunch preparation and eating with Nanny.*
12 noon-2:00pm Daily	*Nap time.*
2:00pm-4:30pm Mondays	*Story hour at the Library with Nanny; stay for crafts.*
2:00pm-4:30pm Tuesdays	*Shopping, errands with Nanny.*
2:00pm-4:30pm Wednesdays	*Play date with friends and Nanny.*
2:00pm-4:30pm Thursdays	*Baking with Nanny.*
2:00pm-4:30pm Fridays	*Reading, quiet play.*
4:30pm-5:30pm Daily	*Snack, bath time, change into night gowns for evening.*
5:30pm-6:00pm Daily	*Dinner preparation with Nanny.* *Dad returns home.*
6:00pm-7:00pm Daily	*Dinner with Dad.*
7:00pm-8:30pm Daily	*Reading with Dad, and bedtime.*

Service Standards: Administrative Standards	
Phone Answering Protocol	*"Good morning/afternoon, Hoyle Residence."*
Door Answering Protocol	*Never open door without knowing who is outside.*
Manner in which family members are addressed	*Mr. Hoyle, Mrs. Templeton, Mr. Rohl, Mrs. Rohl, Meredith, Valerie.*
Manner in which Nanny is addressed	*Nanny.*
Nanny's budget, petty cash	*$2500/month for household, child-related expenses; credit card for unexpected needs.*
Computer	*IBM Clone, Pentium, with 32 Ram, 4.5 Gigs.*
Software	*Windows 95, Microsoft Office, Quicken.*
Day and Time for weekly meetings	*Mondays, 12:30pm-1:30pm.*
Day in the Life	*Friday afternoon.*

SERVICE STANDARDS: Cleaning / Daily Graces Standards	
What are the cleaning standards of the home? Are there any allergies?	*Very high regarding food, dust, sanitation; more relaxed about chores children are learning; allergies are food-related, so cross-contamination of allergens and non-allergenic food is avoided.*
How often does the family have the home cleaned? By whom?	*Daily, housekeeper (30 hours per week).*
What are the Daily Graces to be performed by Nanny?	*These are done with the children, since Anders wants them to learn responsibility:* ☆ *reordering children's room* ☆ *making beds* ☆ *picking up items from the floor* ☆ *collecting children's laundry* ☆ *"search and rescue" of toys from around the house.*
What products are currently used? Are any products not to be used?	*Earth-friendly cleaning supplies when practical; bleach, ammonia, or other toxic substances used sparingly, and kept away from children's reach.*
How often should children's toys, bedrooms, and play areas be cleaned and disinfected? What is the current methodology?	*Nanny disinfects toys during Evening Graces. She uses a solution of diluted Lysol on plastic toys, then rinses. Stuffed animals are washed in the gentle cycle of the washer once a week.*
Who takes care of children's area on the Nanny's days off?	*Dad and children, to varying degrees.*

SERVICE STANDARDS: Cleaning Methodologies	
Children's sheets are changed how often?	*Weekly.*
Mattresses are turned how often?	*Monthly.*
Bedroom is cleaned how often?	*On-going pick-up of toys throughout the day, during the week. Housekeeper vacuums and dusts daily.*
Bedroom is deep cleaned how often? Baseboards dusted, beds moved, light fixtures cleaned, etc.	*Housekeeper deep cleans weekly, moving furniture, cleaning under beds, etc.*
Bathrooms cleaned how often?	*Daily.*
Toys, furniture, fixtures, and accessories are disinfected how often?	*Daily.*
The storage areas for bikes, jet skis, motorcycles, etc. are cleaned and organized how often?	*Housekeeper cleans storage area every other week.*
Closets and drawers cleaned and organized how often?	*Closets are cleaned and organized weekly, outgrown, unworn clothes given away monthly; drawers are straightened as clothes are put away.*
How often are fixtures sterilized? Door knobs, dresser drawer pulls, etc.	*Housekeeper sterilizes doorknobs, telephone receivers, drawer pulls daily.*

SERVICE STANDARDS: Maintenance and Household Hazards — *Baby Proofing*			
Location	**Task to Complete**	**Comp**	**Comments**
Kitchen	Make an inventory of everything in drawers, bin, cabinets, shelves and evaluate for safety	✔	
	Use back burners on stove instead of front when possible	✔	
	Turn handles of pans inward on stove	✔	
	Remove or prevent a swinging door from moving	✔	
	Make the stove, table tops and counter off limits	✔	
	Keep one drawer or cabinet for toys for the child to play with	✔	
	Keep appliances unplugged when not in use	✔	
	Be mindful not to leave utensils within reach while in use	✔	
	Be aware of the child crawling into a space that may close behind them: dryer, refrigerator	✔	
	Keep knives, forks, peelers, or anything sharp out of reach	✔	
	Keep detergents, cleansers, polishes, insecticide, etc. out of reach	✔	
	Keep cords like telephone, appliances, videos out of reach	✔	
Bathroom	Make it off limits to exploration	✔	
	Secure laundry chute	✔	
	Never allow rough housing while bathing	✔	
	Faucet guards to prevent child turning on the water	✔	
	Unplug all appliances	✔	
	Locks too high to reach so children cannot lock themselves in	✔	
	Install non-scalding device	✔	
	Keep razors, scissors, clipper in locked drawers	✔	
	Soaps, shampoos, creams, etc. out of reach	✔	
	Dispose of all out of date medicines and ones not being used	✔	
	Keep all small appliances in a secure place away from water	✔	

SERVICE STANDARDS: Maintenance and Household Hazards — *Baby Proofing*			
Location	**Task to Complete**	**Comp**	**Comments**
Bedroom	Keep cosmetics, deodorants, shoe polish and other poisonous products out of reach	✔	
	Jewelry, beads, buttons, etc. can cause choking if swallowed, keep out of reach and off floor. If choking occurs try to dislodge object, if this is not possible try the Heimlich procedure and call 911	✔	
	Just because items are "out of reach" do not assume that the child cannot get to them; they are very resourceful	✔	
	Fix the lids on any trunks, cedar chest, or similar devices so they do not fall on the child or the child gets locked inside	✔	
Living Room	Look at all chairs, tables, etc. from the child's perspective, getting down on their level helps to see the potential hazards	✔	
General	Make inventory of each room and evaluate its hazard ability	✔	
Room Safety	Wipe up any liquid spills on floor	✔	
Tips	Assess bookcases for sturdiness	✔	
	Secure furniture with tops that open so children do not injure hands and fingers and do not risk suffocating	✔	
	Make a barrier in front of radiators, floor furnaces, fireplaces	✔	
	Stairs should have a gate in front of them if there are babies or toddlers in the home	✔	
	Keep plants of any kind out of reach; many are poisonous	✔	
	Be cautious of small objects like hard candy, cigarette butts, etc. that can be swallowed	✔	
	Keep all cords, extensions, lamps, appliances, blinds, phones, etc. wound up and out of reach	✔	
	Keep all electronic equipment out of reach	✔	
	Keep all alcohol cabinets securely locked; install cabinet locks	✔	
	Purchase outlet covers for all outlets	✔	
	Use corner guards on all furniture, cabinets, especially glass tables	✔	
	Place nonskid strips on rugs and in bathtubs to prevent falling	✔	
	Purchase lead paint detector kits	✔	
	Keep all matches, lighters, etc. away from children	✔	
	Make sure basement or stair accesses are locked or gated	✔	
	Halogen lamps get hot very quickly; keep them out of reach	✔	

SERVICE STANDARDS: Property and Grounds Standards	
How much land surrounds the home?	*2 acres.*
Is there a pool, do the children swim? Is it gated?	*Yes, with child-safety locks; also children have been given swimming lessons from age of 6 months.*
What areas could be seen as hazardous to the children?	*Garage, laundry room, storage area for cleaning supplies. Dad's darkroom.*
Are there pets, are they child sensitive?	*Cat is very tolerant. Children taught how to handle cat and gerbil, and not to handle the fish!*
When are children allowed outside?	*Only with adult supervision, during day.*
Is there a designated playground?	*Swing, climbing area, slide, in sheltered corner of side yard, which is gated.*
Are there areas where children are not allowed?	*Dad's darkroom (lock on door, and doorknob placed 5 feet high).*
Are there busy streets nearby?	*No, quiet lanes in immediate area, low traffic; cul-de-sacs.*

SERVICE STANDARDS: Clothing Standards	
Describe Clothing Standards. How do you want your children dressed? For play, for school, for entertaining, for church?	*Children wear overalls, rompers, for play; not yet in school; designer dresses for entertaining and church.*
What part does your child play in choosing clothing, dressing and clothes care?	*Child is given options selected by Nanny from which to choose outfit for day or event.*
How many loads of children's laundry per week? Done by whom? What days?	*8-10 loads of laundry done by Housekeeper and Nanny per week. Dad runs occasional load on the weekends.*
What clothing typically do you want ironed or hand washed?	*Dresses require ironing, sweaters and other woolens require hand washing.*
What detergent/s and fabric softeners are used on the children's clothes?	*Ivory Snow used for children's washable clothes, no fabric softener (causes a rash on children).*
Who purchases the child's clothing?	*Nanny (for clothes worn at Dad's house) and Mother, grandmother.*
What look do you want the child to have and when?	*For play, Dad prefers them to "look like normal kids," for dress, he prefers designer items, ribbons in hair.*
What is the child designer that you buy the most of?	*Christian Dior.*
Are there any special instructions on what is used to clean the child's clothes?	*No, other than above; otherwise following label instructions.*
What dry cleaner do you use for the children's clothing?	*Scott's Earth-Friendly Dry Cleaners.*
How are the clothes disposed of when the child no longer wears them?	*Given to church or other charity.*

SERVICE STANDARDS: Clothing Standards	
How is the child's closet to be organized?	*Dividers, double rows of hanging clothes, shelves, drawers.*
What type of shoes does the child wear?	*For play: Reeboks, for dress: Buster Brown.*
How are shoes disposed of when the child can no longer wear them?	*Charity.*

Service Standards: Cooking Standards	
"Healthy and growing—it starts with good nutrition"	
What are the cooking Family Standards or Family Cooking Style	*Low-fat, high protein, avoidance of allergenic foods.*
Example of Household Menus	*Breakfast: Lean turkey sausage, fruit, non-sugared cereal for children, with Rice Milk.* *Lunch: Cashew butter sandwiches, lean meats (turkey burgers), broccoli flowerettes, fruit.* *Dinner: Broiled fish, vegetables, salad.*
Dietary restrictions	*No milk, eggs, whole wheat products, peanuts.*
Favorite foods	*Ice cream (Rocky Road), Tofu or Rice Dream version.*
Kitchen standards	*Sanitizing of counters after every meal.*
Use of special equipment	*Bread maker for non-allergenic breads.*
Healthy Snacks	*Vegetables, cheese, low-fat granola bars, fruit.*
Style of presentation	*Formal for family dinners, simple for children.*
Table etiquette	*Children being taught family's standards at every meal.*
Clean up	*Housekeeper for breakfast and lunch; Nanny for dinner.*
Meal times	*6:30 a.m., 11:30 a.m. and 6:00 p.m.*
Guests at regular meals	*Extended family on Sunday afternoons.*

SERVICE STANDARDS: Cooking and Children's Meal Preparations	
What are meal times for the children?	6:30 a.m. with Dad daily, lunch 11:30 a.m. with Nanny, and Dinner is 6:00 p.m. with Dad.
What are snack times for the children?	After morning walk and 4ish in the afternoon.
Who prepares the children's meals?	Nanny.
What style of cooking do you want for the children?	Healthy, careful of allergies, no processed foods, lots of fruits and vegetables.
What type of snacks can the children have?	Low-fat granola bars, fruit, dried and fresh, cheese. No fried or processed foods. Check ingredients.
Can the children have desserts or other sweets? If so what?	Occasional home baked cookies, cakes and ice cream.
Where do the children eat?	Breakfast room for breakfast and lunch. Dining room for dinner.
What is the child's favorite foods?	Meredith: custard (egg-free/milk-free). Valerie: tapioca pudding (egg-free/milk-free).
What is the child's favorite snack?	Granola bars.

SERVICE STANDARDS: Entertaining Standards	
"Good manners and knowledge of etiquette are as important as anything a youngster can learn." - *Tiffany's Table Manners*	
What are the entertaining standards of the household?	*Casual but well mannered. Children always well dressed, mostly family oriented. Formally set table for Sunday dinners. Often will invite neighbors, photography friends, buffets, barbeques and pool parties in the summer.*
Are there family dinners?	*Yes, nightly when the children are with Dad and on Sundays.*
How is the family dinner table usually set?	*Set for 3 course meals. Stainless Steel for everyday, silver on Sundays. No paper napkins or plates ever!*
Style of table service?	*Plated service. Occasional Russian Service on holidays or other special family Sunday dinners.*
What kind of parties do the children usually attend?	*Family occasions and birthday parties of their friends.*
What kind of parties do the children usually give?	*Birthday parties and Sunday tea parties with Grandmother.*
What is household protocol when children's guests are present?	*Meredith and/or Valerie are treated as hostesses.*
Do's of table manners Don'ts of table manners	
What do children wear when you are entertaining?	*Appropriate for event, but usually party dresses.*
Where can children entertain?	*In Family Room.*
Describe the style of entertaining for birthdays.	

SERVICE STANDARDS: Children's Entertaining	
Favorite seasons - holidays - special occasions (How are they usually celebrated?)	With full decorum.
Favorite flowers, decorations or themes for entertaining - types of party favors, colors, textures, etc.	Dad likes fresh flowers in the home, lilies and white roses are his favorites. Favors must be safe for children under three.
Most enjoyable types of parties	
Menus most enjoyed	
Numbers of guests; ages	5 children; any number of adults.
Frequency of both large and small gatherings	Weekly.
What activities, games are favorites?	
Describe the children's portrait of the "best party" they ever attended.	
What's the favorite party beverage?	Punch bowl filled with seltzer plus floating sorbet.
What part should the adults play in a children's party?	Observers, not focal point.
What part do the children play in the adult's party?	Children are not expected to participate in or enjoy the adult conversations, so they are provided with other activities.
Who accompanies the children to the party? Who attends the party, the parent or the Nanny?	Mother or Father, if available; Nanny at other times.
Who writes the RSVP?	Nanny, if invitation is sent to Dad.
Who purchases the gift?	Mother or Nanny.

SERVICE STANDARDS: Transportation & Travel	
Security concern	*Automobile and pool safety. Children never left alone.*
Agent - phone	
Favorite hotels and facilities	*Disney World.*
Preferred accommodations with children	*Must order crib for Valerie.*
Packing checklist	*1. Proper day time clothing per weather reports* *2. Night time clothing* *3. Diapers, handi-wipes* *4. Bottles, snacks, juice* *5. Extra change of clothing* *6. Quiet play toys/books/games* *7. Car seat for Valerie on the plane.*
Travel activities	*Check with Hotel Concierge for child appropriate activities. Favorite books, stuffed animals and blankets.*
Foods recommended for children during travel activities	*Avoid allergenic foods wherever possible.*
Who drives children to school daily?	
Which car is used to transport children?	*Range Rover.*
What route is used to go to school?	
What other children activities require transportation?	*Play dates, errands with Nanny.*
Car seat and seat belt requirements and for which children?	*Both children have car seats.*
Who is insurance carrier? If accident, what steps to follow?	
Have children's special meals been ordered from the airline?	

SERVICE STANDARDS: Travel and Nanny Checklist for International Travel	
Medical insurance for the family or the Nanny covered outside the United States? What coverage will there be, otherwise?	*Aetna for emergency medical for entire family. Special rider required when leaving country.*
What provisions are made for time off for the Nanny during the trip?	*One week or less, compensatory time off when trip is completed. Longer trips will provide two days off per week on site.*
If the Nanny flies in different part of the plane from the parents, what coverage will be provided for her rest room breaks?	*Parents to provide relief every two hours.*
Does the Nanny have a credit card and sufficient petty cash to cover tips, cab fares, meals in resort locations?	*Yes, Master Card, only to be used as emergency supplement. Travelers' checks and cash provided daily.*
Have emergency numbers for pediatrician been obtained, for approval of any medicines prescribed in other countries?	*Yes, in suitcase, in diaper bag, and in Nanny's purse.*
What are the guidelines for room service, mini-bars, other food expenses?	*Discussed with parents.*
Have guest business cards been ordered from hotel(s) for Nanny and children, in order to identify them and to protect their home address?	*Ordered from Concierge.*
Have copies been made of passports, given to a relative in the U.S., and carried in separate place while traveling?	*Yes, given to grandparents.*
Have regulations regarding visas and travel restrictions for Nannies been clarified?	*Yes.*
If the children are to stay in Nanny's room, will she be paid for her additional coverage, and/or given additional time off?	*Discussed with parents.*

SERVICE STANDARDS: Security and Children's Special Concerns	
What are the special concerns regarding the safety and security of your children?	*Pool, dark room and supplies.*
Are there custody, visitation or other legal agreements?	*Shared custody.*
How often are the children to play outside?	*Daily, with supervision.*
If outside play is frequent, are children to use sun screen (what brand and where is it located?) Or wear hats, etc.?	*Shade SPF 45, plus hats.*
Is there a complete first-aid kit in the car used to transport the children?	*In all cars.*
What have the children been told regarding the issue of strangers and how to handle those situations?	*Children have been instructed to call out, "Stranger!" in these situations of attempted abduction.*
To what destinations must the children be accompanied?	*All.*
How are play dates to be arranged?	*Nanny arranges them.*
Are there any particular facility hazards of concern to the parents, e.g. a pool with a low fence, construction on the property, wells, drainage systems, accessible tools?	*Neighbors have no fence around their Koi pond.*
If the children may leave the home unaccompanied, where may they go and how may they be contacted if needed?	*N/A*
Are tree houses permitted?	*Not yet.*
To what degree may the children get 'dirty'?	*To a fair degree, within normal limits.*
How often are the children's toys and outside and inside play areas inspected for damage/repairs?	*Children bring them, one-by-one to Nanny for a "check-up," and Nanny uses the opportunity to enhance their observation skills.*

SERVICE STANDARDS: Children's Education/Care Standards—*For the Parents*	
What educational philosophy would you like followed?	*Lifelong love of learning, intellectual curiosity.*
What types of crafts does your child like?	*Anything art related!*
What types of books does your child like, are there favorites? Are there favorites for bedtime?	*Picture books, story books.* *Meredith: The Velveteen Rabbit.* *Valerie: Curious George.*
What kind of physical activities would you like your child to participate in?	*Would like them to try many kinds of activities, to find which ones suit them best.*
Is your child athletic? How?	*Wonderful swimmers!*
Is your child musically inclined? Are there favorite bedtime songs that you like to have sung?	*Meredith can pick out the notes of songs on the piano, simply by hearing them. Meredith: Rock-a Bye Baby.* *Valerie: Twinkle, Twinkle, Little Star.*
Is your child artistic? How?	*Both children demonstrate a good sense of color and interest in art.*
What are your child's sleeping patterns?	*The children sleep soundly, from 8:30 p.m. until awakened by Dad at 6:30 a.m.*
What educational goals do you have for your child in the next month? For the next year?	*Meredith: Mastery of the alphabet and letter sounds; reading beginning books by the end of the year. Valerie: Learning her colors; on-going vocabulary expansion and increasing verbal skills.*

SERVICE STANDARDS: Educational Service Standards—*To the Children*	
Do you like to attend school? If so what school do you like to attend?	
Do you have a favorite teacher or teachers?	
Do you like to read? If so what do you like to read? How often do you like to read?	*The children love stories, and being read to! Meredith loves fantasy stories, such as Velveteen Rabbit and fairy tales. Valerie loves Curious George and Good Night, Moon.*
What are your favorite educational activities?	*The children say they like the interactive Arthur books for the computer.*
What type of videos or movies do you like to watch?	*The children like Disney videos, or Veggie Tales.*
What type of TV programs do you like to watch? How often do you like to watch TV or videos?	*No TV allowed!*
How often do you play at friends' homes? Are there rules regarding when and where you are able to play at other homes?	
How often do you like to use the computer? Do you know how to access the Internet? What are the home guidelines regarding your access?	
When do you like to do your homework? What is your favorite subject?	
Who would you like to sign your notes from school?	
What have you been told about staying away from "strangers" and how would you handle this type of situation?	
What have you been taught about what things are right or wrong? What things do you think are right or wrong?	
Do you know how to swim?	*Yes!*
What have you been taught or do you know about things in and out of the house that are unsafe? What steps do you take to keep yourself from getting hurt?	

SERVICE STANDARDS. Educational Service Standards—*To the Children*	
What responsibilities do you have in keeping your area clean? What things do you like to do? What things don't you like to do?	*The children help the Nanny with her Graces; they love "Search and Rescue" of their toys scattered around the house. Meredith does not like folding her laundered clothes or putting them away. Valerie does not like to straighten the blankets on her crib.*
What is your favorite music, favorite songs or musical instruments?	*The children love to play the piano.*
What are the rules about bicycles or other outside moving recreational toys?	*The children can only use them with supervision.*
Is there a school or play schedule and events calendar?	*The Nanny keeps the play schedule on her calendar.*
Do you have subscriptions or newspapers or books that are regularly ordered and received?	*The children are members of a children's book club, and receive Highlights.*
What sports are favorites? What sports event have you attended?	*The children have been to a basketball game.*

Day in the Life Schedules

Employers of the nineties typically are used to and appreciate pre-planning, particularly in written form. The established Day in the Life structure allows everyone in the house to participate in the household routine. Employers know which day the piano teacher comes and which day the children's clothing is washed, so they can pull out the shirt that has a small spot on it from the weekend, that might otherwise go unseen, and the Nanny knows that special treatment might be needed for the shirt or a written inventory needs to be prepared prior to taking it to the dry cleaner. The employer knows which days are baking days and looks forward to the smells within the house and to having special treats with the children. You also know what days the heavy cleaning is being accomplished in the kitchen. That would not be the best day to invite the neighborhood kids over.

Examples of Day in the Life daily activities are examined in the next few pages. Note that each day has morning and evening "Daily Graces" and a specific style of work. This consistency helps everyone know what is being done and provides for support of these activities. The idea is to be pro-active in work, not reactive! A pro-active style creates a weekly schedule of expected daily activities. Day in the Life schedules should be completed the week prior to the schedule and submitted to the family for reference and approval. These may be handwritten, or the use of *The Household Manager's Software* will greatly enhance your ability to complete these quickly and efficiently. If the Day in the Life schedules are in place when a "Master the Moment" event requires a different service or special duty, the employer will know what may not have gotten done that day. In addition the employer can make conscious choices and evaluate how the Nanny spends time. We call this "fine-tuning" the Day in the Life.

This begins the process of providing an overall structure to the Nanny and to the daily lives of the children. Communication with employer(s) needs to occur weekly and on an as-needed basis. For each day we recommend allocating some time for this.

☆ 88 ☆

On the following pages are examples of Nanny's Day in the Life schedules. We have continued the example of the single father and have added two additional examples for your reference. Three different scenarios were chosen to demonstrate that no two Day in the Life situations are the same. Each household has unique Service Standards, different priorities, and individual family preferences.

Remember – the higher the structure, the higher the service delivery.

DAY IN THE LIFE OF THE NANNY — EXAMPLE 1

Single Parent, Live-In Nanny

Week of:	Date:
Time	**Activities**
7:30am-8:00am Daily	Nanny takes over with children, as Dad leaves for work. Nanny helps children select clothing and dress, brush teeth, comb hair and have breakfast.
8:00am-10:00am Daily	Housekeeper arrives daily. Nanny and children do appropriate child-related Graces including: ☆ Reordering children's room, making beds, picking up items from the floor. ☆ Gathering children's laundry for morning load(s), folding and putting away. ☆ Picking up toys, and child-related items from the other parts of the house.
10:00am-11:30am Daily	Morning walk with children, outside play, weather permitting. If not, reading, indoor play
11:30am-12noon Daily	Lunch preparation and eating. Meredith and Valerie can "help" Nanny to prepare what they eat. Nanny and children have lunch.
12noon-2:00pm Daily	Children take naps. **Monday:** weekly meeting with Father to discuss week's priorities, Day in the Life Schedules, Nanny's performance, children's needs etc. **Tuesday:** Nanny confirms or arranges play dates, other outside activities. Checks with Mother or Mother's Nanny to confirm schedules. *Or Nanny uses opportunity to have a break, then does leftover chores from morning, additional laundry, etc. *Meredith usually awakens sooner, so she plays quietly until Valerie is awake. Housekeeper leaves at 1:00pm.
2:00pm to 4:30pm Mondays	Nanny takes children to the Library, for story hour, checking out books with children. Stay for craft hour.
2:00pm-4:30pm Tuesdays	Nanny uses afternoon for errands and grocery shopping for family, taking children with her.
2:00pm-4:30pm Wednesdays	Play date for Meredith and/or Valerie. Friends come over, trade visits, so that children go to friends' homes. Nanny attends play dates with children. Talks with other Nannies.
2:00pm-4:30pm Thursdays	Baking day! Children love to spend time in the kitchen. They bake bread, make gingerbread cookies and honor holidays with special goodies.

Week of:	Date:
Time	**Activities**
2:00pm-4:30pm Fridays	*Reading or quiet play time for the children in their play room. Nanny creates next week's Day in the Life for submission to Dad for his reference and approval. Checks with Mother or Mother's Nanny for schedules.*
4:30pm-5:30pm Daily	*Snack, bath time, change into night gowns for evening.*
5:30pm-6:00pm Daily	*Dinner preparation, Dad returns home.*
6:00pm-6:30pm Daily	*Evening Graces:* *Going throughout house, retrieving toys and other child-related items, and returning them to their room* *Reordering children's room* *Completes laundry, as needed* *Doing any residual dishes from the day*
6:30pm-7:00pm Daily	*Nanny has her own dinner.*
7:00pm Daily	*Nanny returns to her quarters. Takes a weekly class in the evenings, sees a movie with other Nannies in the neighborhood or works out.*

Notes:

If Dad has date or evening business meeting, etc., Nanny is scheduled and contracted separately to watch children.

When children at Mom's, Nanny takes days to clean closets, inventories and sanitizes toys, rotating those that are no longer of interest, also sorting children's clothing, taking unused to the donation site, attending special classes in child development or computer classes. Also will schedule and supervise repairs and vendors doing work in the home.

Principals: *Dad works full time, owns his company, wants a loving, stable atmosphere for children in his absence. He has shared custody of children with Mom living in same community.*

Children: *Meredith, age 4; Valerie, age 2*
Quality playtime important to Dad; he wants children not to watch television. Nanny is currently teaching colors and numbers to Valerie, alphabet and letter-recognition to Meredith.

Nanny: *Lives in separate apartment area within the home, separate entrance and efficiency kitchen.*

Staff: *Full-time Nanny, part-time Housekeeper, who works 30 hours/week*

Home: *5,000 Sq. Ft. Home*

Day in the Life of the Nanny — Example 2

Staffed Home, Stay-at-Home Mom

Week of:	Date:
Time	**Activities**
8:00am-8:15am Tuesdays - Saturdays	*Start; communication time with Mrs., priorities, schedule changes, special child needs.*
8:15am - 9:30am Tuesdays - Saturdays	*Overseeing breakfast for Brian, giving Natalie cereal. Preparing Brian for pre-school during the week or for Saturday's fun; dressing him and Natalie. Return home with Natalie to begin Morning Graces. Mom works out with personal trainer while Nanny is gone with children.*
9:30am - 12:00 noon Tuesdays - Saturdays	*Mom with Natalie for morning. Nanny does Daily Graces:* ☆ *Reordering nursery, making Brian's bed, and changing or straightening crib covers.* ☆ *Walking house to retrieve child-related items which have been scattered in various places.* ☆ *Start laundry of children's clothes.* ☆ *Preparation of Natalie's bottles for day.* ☆ *Nanny picks up Brian during the week at pre-school; Natalie stays with Mom.*
12:00 noon-12:30pm Tuesdays - Saturdays	*Mrs. and Nanny have lunch with children. (Cook provides and serves lunch.)*
12:30pm to 2:00pm Tuesdays - Saturdays	*Naps for both children and while they are napping:* **Tuesday:** *Nanny plans menus for the week, creates children's grocery list for cook, folding diapers, additional laundry.* **Wednesday:** *Nanny meets with HM and other staff to coordinate household and children's schedules.* **Thursday:** *Sanitizes children's toys, sort out grown clothing and prepare for donations.* **Friday:** *Organize children's clothing, iron, hand wash special dresses or pack for travel.* **Saturday:** *Nanny plans and submits her next week Day in the Life schedules for mom's approval.*
2:00pm-4:30pm Tuesdays	*At-home day, for children to read, play educational games, outdoor play, weather permitting.*
2:00pm-4:30pm Wednesdays	*Invite children's play mates for afternoon crafts, play activities, games, etc., another child may come home from pre-school with Brian. Mom does volunteer work at local hospital.*
2:00pm-4:30pm Thursdays	*Trip to the Park, Zoo, or Nature walk with Brian; Natalie in stroller or other outside activity with both children. Mother occasionally accompanies Nanny.*

Week of:	Date:
Time	**Activities**
2:00pm-4:30pm Fridays	*Quiet time at home for children. Nanny supports looking at books, playing with toys.*
2:00pm-4:30pm Saturdays	*Extended family gatherings, neighborhood friends or other casual weekend entertaining typically takes place.*
4:30pm- 5:00pm Tuesdays-Saturdays	*Healthy snack for children. Begin winding down from day's activities.*
5:00pm-5:30pm Tuesdays-Saturdays	*Bath time for children, dress for bed.*
5:30pm-7:00pm Tuesdays-Saturdays	*Children have extended dinner with parents (unless the parents have other plans). Nanny supports with feeding of Natalie, if needed. Otherwise, Nanny performs Evening Graces:* ☆ *Reordering nursery.* ☆ *Walking house to retrieve children's items.* ☆ *Finishing laundry, putting away clothes, setting out clothes for following day.* ☆ *Preparing bottles as back-up for Natalie, if needed, during night.* ☆ *Nanny confirms following day's activities, confirming play dates, task lists for errands, etc.*
7:00pm-7:30pm Tuesdays-Saturdays	*Nanny returns to her quarters for evening, unless special arrangements have been made for after-hours care.*
Sundays, Mondays	*Notes: Typical schedule for P.T. Nanny as above schedule for full-time Nanny. Also many Saturdays, the Nanny may do outside errands, while P.T. Nanny covers with children.*
Principals:	*Mom and Dad, Dad manages investments, Mother stay-at-home, breast-feeds Natalie, is very child-oriented, interested in quality time with children. Mom volunteers 1 afternoon per week at local Hospital.*
Children:	*Brian, aged 2; Natalie, aged 4 months.*
Nanny:	*Lives in separate apartment over the garage.*
Home:	*12,000 Square Foot home*
Staff:	*Full-time H M, full-time Cook, f-t Housekeeper, f-t Nanny and p.t. Nanny for 7 day/wk coverage. Part-time Nanny performs evening childcare when parents are traveling or when parents have guests or evenings out, and Saturdays through Mondays to support. Nanny supervises and trains this Nanny.*

DAY IN THE LIFE OF THE NANNY — EXAMPLE 3

Live-Out Nanny, Both Parents Work

Week of:	Date:
Time	**Activities**
7:00am - 7:15am Daily	*Communication time with Mrs., talk about Sam's school report. Discuss children's activities with parent.*
7:15am - 8:00am Daily	*Wake, bathe and dress Sam - support Becky's dressing as needed. Make breakfast, cereal, toast, fruit and juice for children and have breakfast. Nanny cuts up fruit the night before.*
8:00am - 9:00am Alternates Daily	*Children ride to school with neighbor (Nanny drives car pool on Tues. and Thurs.). When driving car pool, it takes approximately 1 hour out of day.*
9:00am - 11:00am Daily	*Daily Graces to include opening of house. Clean breakfast dishes, bring home back to a state of order, make beds, gather laundry, freshen baths. When driving, Daily Graces occur 1 hour later.*
11:00am - 12:00 noon Alternates Daily	*Monday, Wednesday and Friday, sort clothing, put in load of laundry, iron children's good clothing, put away laundry. Also change beds on Wednesdays.*
12:00 noon - 1:00pm Daily	*Prepare children's lunch. Mondays organize menus for parents' approval for Tuesday shopping. Tuesdays through Fridays during this time Nanny to plan Day in the Life schedules, plan menus, organize play activities, museum trips, etc.*
1:00pm - 2:00pm Daily	*Sam and Becky return home from pre-school (dropped off by car pool). Nanny and children have lunch. Talk/time with Sam and Becky, find out about day, check for home work. Put children down for short nap or quiet time.*
2:00pm-4:30pm Mondays	*At home play time for the children, numbers, crafts, alphabet and Nanny reading with the children.*
2:00pm - 4:30pm Tuesdays	*Weekly errands, Grocery shopping, library for books and video store for children's movies.*
2:00pm - 4:30pm Wednesdays	*Developed at home activities such as baking cookies, gymnastics, or invite children's play mates for afternoon crafts.*
2:00pm - 4:30pm Thursdays	*Trip to the children's museum or the neighborhood park playground with children's friends.*

Week of:	Date:
Time	**Activities**
2:00pm - 4:30pm Fridays	*Ready household for weekend activities, children help plan for suggested outings for weekend with parents. Quiet Time for children, reading, numbers and alphabet, playing quietly.*
4:30pm- 5:00pm Daily	*Very light healthy snack. Nanny and children provide Evening Graces, close curtains, pick up toys, set table and bring house back to a state of order.*
5:00pm - 7:00pm Daily	*Prep work for dinner, kids playing at the kitchen counter, doing "home work" or coloring. Parents arrive 5:30-6:00pm. Nanny leaves for evening.*

Notes:

Principals: *Mom and Dad both corporate executives. Lots of clothing utilized and appearance of children important priority to family.*

Children: *Becky and Sam, ages 5 and 3.*

Home: *3,000 Square Feet.*

Nanny: *Full-time Nanny, lives out, (apartment about 10 minutes away)*

Staff: *Full-time Nanny supported by one day (7 hours) per week House Cleaner.*

Creating a Service Culture

Nannies see their value as professionals
and perform accordingly.

As educators, we want to complete this process by sharing some how-to's for creating positive relationships and techniques to manage Nannies. We assume that the person you have hired has the essential professional qualifications for Nannying. Candidates who have never been Nannies before and who have not obtained any form of training in Nannying or child development are generally very poor risks. Starkey's qualifications for Nannies are based on the clients that we serve. However, each parent will want to make their own decisions based on their individual needs, the level of responsibility, and the available supervision.

Starkey's Professional Career Nanny Qualifications

- ☆ We feel a minimum age of twenty-five is required to be placed as a Career Nanny.

- ☆ At least four references have been contacted personally by the agent or by the employer family. References should be former positions and long-term family friends.

- ☆ A minimum of three years progressive household experience working as a babysitter, mother's helper or Nanny.

- ☆ Educational experience in basic child development methods and play activities. We recommend at least two years or the equivalent additional in-home experience.

- ☆ A clean background check. Contact an investigative firm to perform criminal, social security and driving background checks.
- ☆ Has demonstrated emotional maturity and is able to prove responsible behavior in prior work situations.
- ☆ Ability to articulate their style of Nannying, childcare philosophy and techniques, verbally or in writing.

Mrs. Starkey's Nanny Manager states that each household has a particular image and personality. Family personalities are manifested and supported through the household's Favorites, Service Standards and Day in the Life schedules. To come full circle, Nannies require:

- ☆ A vision of the parents' expectations
- ☆ Communication with the parents
- ☆ Regular patterns in daily duties

Most service providers are visual in nature when communicating. As a personality type, they most easily feel what is needed or they see what is needed. They often work intuitively and by observation rather than from an academic perspective. Talking directly with the parents at regularly scheduled times under a pre-set itinerary works best. Both the parents and the Nanny are better able to focus their attention. Scheduled, uninterrupted weekly meetings apart from the children are essential. It is very important for parents and Nannies to crystallize child development goals, educational priorities, play activities, menus, behaviors, and discipline. Performance reviews would also be included in these meetings.

Held weekly, these meetings will create a synergy between the parents and the Nanny, create a sense of professionalism, and will send the message that the parents value the Nanny and the service provided. It also reminds both the parents and the Nanny that this is an employer/employee relationship.

When training the Nanny about the type of childcare activities, sanitizing of toys, organization of closets or setting up play dates, etc. parents are more successful if they demonstrate or have the prior Nanny demonstrate how it should be done. It is essential that information and standards be communicated clearly. Nannies should welcome the participation and feedback of the parent who is observing the Nanny's techniques. This should occur early on to create good working patterns. Active participation with parents also fosters mutual confidence and provides the Nanny an opportunity to succeed. Parents and Nannies need to be respectful and vocal about what is and is not working. Again this should be communicated during regular weekly communication meetings. Lists or short conversations in the morning before the parents walk out the door are helpful but should not replace weekly meetings. For additional communication techniques, utilize voice-activated tape recorders, cell phones or pagers for both Nannies and parents.

We have also discovered that utilizing formal surnames when communicating on a regular basis (Mr. and Mrs.) is essential etiquette in this industry. This small formality creates a more gracious communication mode. Household employment offers little or no formal boundaries in which to promote professionalism; without some subtle reminders, it soon falls away.

It typically takes approximately three to six months to fully communicate all household standards and nuances, and to set up a childcare service delivery system. So, finding the right match of Nanny and family preserves quality of life for everyone. Allow enough time for the alchemy of a service relationship to grow and mature. The result is worth its weight in gold!

SOME WORDS ABOUT LISTENING!

To Parents:

- ☆ Are your children happy?

- ☆ Do your children share information that reflect Day in the Life schedules?

- ☆ When conducting these meetings, are you listening carefully?

- ☆ Is your Nanny able to communicate to you what is occurring with your children?

- ☆ Is the conversation open and genuine?

- ☆ Expect completed Day in the Life schedules for the following week.

- ☆ Do the Day in the Life schedules accurately reflect what is taking place?

- ☆ Is the Nanny able to share the good and the bad with you?

- ☆ Are your children the focus of the conversations?

- ☆ Are there other issues that need to be worked out?

To Nannies:

- ☆ Are you enjoying your time with the children?

- ☆ Do you laugh with the children, and have fun?

- ☆ Do you feel as though your days have some structure or do you feel you are in a crisis mode?

- ☆ Do you have planning time for creating your Day in the Life schedules, menus, etc?

- ☆ Listen to yourself; are you fighting for control or building a mutually positive relationship with the children? With the parents?

- ☆ Are the children open with you and do they want to engage you in conversation?

- ☆ Are you on your employer's agenda?

- ☆ Are the weekly meetings open, genuine, and are your questions heard and answered?

> **These meetings provide the Communication. They include the Vision or the Service Standards. They provide the Regular Patterns carried out through the Day in the Life schedules.**

PUTTING IT ALL TOGETHER

For some time Starkey International has been teaching our Nanny Management System in our Starkey Nanny Advancement Program (S.N.A.P.), and with our clients who have hired our Nannies. The response has been overwhelmingly positive. When the Day in the Life schedules are completed, Nannies and parents are amazed at what they see. We have observed that even the veteran professionals light up with a newfound sense of consciousness. They are charged with renewed energy. They experience with great delight, a new understanding of their role and what they actually accomplish each day. They genuinely realize their value as a professional. It is wonderful to watch this transformation occur.

Nannies, until they complete this process, have a difficult time recognizing the part they play within a home and how they are able to affect an entire family — either positively or negatively. Nannies begin to see themselves as professionals and perform accordingly. One of the most important benefits of the Nanny Manager System is that Nannies learn they are in a service role to the family and are able to see the opportunity and fully take pride in it.

Choosing to be a Nanny is choosing service as a profession.

Parents also learn a great deal from the Nanny Management System. They find out what the Nanny does all day, minute by minute. They find that they are able to take a greater part in the creation of the everyday lives of their children. Of most importance, they discover what they are asking another to do. The employer is also able to practically ascertain if additional household help is needed. It helps the entire household become more functional in their everyday work. Through mutual understanding, the Nanny Management System helps create a relationship in the most positive way.

Children respond with enthusiasm to the consistency and stability within the home. They feel special that they are asked what is important to them, and that their particular favorites are recognized. They also watch their parents and the Nanny mutually create their daily experience, and are not able to make either the parent or the Nanny "the bad person" for requiring a particular behavior and expecting a family standard.

Many parents feel they are able to give this book to the Nanny and the transformation will occur. This will not generally be the case. *It is impossible for the Nanny to complete the process without the participation of the parent.* It takes a partnership. If the parents would like their household and Nanny to perform with their vision, then they must fully impart their vision.

PARENTS -

Paint the picture

Share your standards

Help your Nanny become a Nanny Manager!

Additional Workbook Forms

The following are additional forms that are helpful in the management and care of children. To implement Mrs. Starkey's Nanny Management System and create your own Nanny Manager Book, you may order a full set of Nanny Manager Forms. Call the Starkey corporate offices toll-free at 1-877-STARKEY (782-7539).

FAMILY INFORMATION

Father	
Employer	
Secretary/Assistant	
Address	
Work Phone	Mobile Phone
Work Schedule:	
Monday	Thursday
Tuesday	Friday
Wednesday	
Chronic Health Conditions	
Allergies	
Medications	
Height	Weight
Hair color	Eye Color
Blood Type	
Primary Physician	
Address	
Phone	Answering Service
Additional Treating Physicians	
Special Medical Needs	
Insurance Company	
Address	
I.D.	Phone Number

FAMILY INFORMATION

Mother	
Employer	
Secretary/Assistant	
Address	
Work Phone	Mobile Phone
Work Schedule:	
Monday	Thursday
Tuesday	Friday
Wednesday	
Chronic Health Conditions	
Allergies	
Medications	
Height	Weight
Hair color	Eye Color
Blood Type	
Primary Physician	
Address	
Phone	Answering Service
Additional Treating Physicians	
Special Medical Needs	
Insurance Company	
Address	
I.D.	Phone

FAMILY INFORMATION

Child

School

Teacher/s

Address

School Phone

Nanny

Activity Schedule:

Monday	Thursday
Tuesday	Friday
Wednesday	

Chronic Health Conditions

Allergies

Medications

| Height | Weight |
| Hair color | Eye Color |

Blood Type

Pediatrician

Address

Phone

Answering Service

Insurance Company

Address

| I.D. | Phone Number |

NANNY/BABYSITTER INFORMATION

Date Created	
Family	
Address	
Nearest Intersection	
Location and address where parents will be	Phone
Home Phone	
Work Phone (father)	Mother
Cellular Phone (father)	Mother
Neighbor(s)	
Address	Phone
Close friend	Phone
Police Fire Department	Ambulance
Medical Emergencies - Hospital	
Poison Control	
Children's doctor	
Address	Phone
Pharmacy	
Address	Phone
Hospital	
Address	Phone
Insurance policy	Number
Dentist	
Address	Phone
Instructions:	

HOUSEHOLD SAFETY & SECURITY INFORMATION

Family		
Address		
Phone Number		
Electrical breaker box location		
Water cutoff		
Thermostats		
Alarm System Monitoring Co.		
Smoke Detectors		
Fire Extinguishers		
Fire Exit Route Plan		
First Aid Kit Location		
Alarm System Key Pad Location		
Neighbor	Neighbor	
Address	Address	
Phone	Phone	
Pediatrician	Phone (Day)	(Night)
Family Physician	Phone (Day)	(Night)
Dentist	Phone (Day)	(Night)
Insurance Co.	Phone	
Address		
Policy Number		
Mother's Work		
Cell phone #		
Father's Work		
Cell phone #		

HEALTH AND SAFETY

"The number one concern of parents today is the health and safety of their children." Report from survey by *Family Circle* Magazine

Doctor/s - addresses, phones	
Dentist - address, phone	
Family Pharmacy - address, phone	
Hospital - address, phone	
Orthodontist - address, phone	
Allergies to medications?	
Insurance policy information	
Poison Control	
Relative or Friend in case of Emergency	
Car Pools, who and when?	
Extra House key	
Alarm System Monitoring Company	
Alarm System Key Pad Instructions	

HOUSEHOLD / CHILDREN'S VENDORS

Grocery Store	
Shoe Repair	
Dry Cleaners	
Tailor	
Clothing Store	
Movie Rentals	
Library Cards	
Internet Access	
Ice Cream Parlor	
School	
Church	

SERVICES		
Vendor	**Name**	**Address/Phone**
Laundry Delivery		
Auto Club		
Exterminator Service person Scheduled Service		
Children's Haircuts Stylist-		
TV/VCR Repair		
Cleaning Service Service Person Scheduled Service		
Tailor		
Handyman		
Shoe Repair		
Pharmacy		
Pharmacists		
Insurance Delivery		
Movie Rental- Card #		

DRY CLEANING FORM

Name	Normal Day/time of pickup
Address	Normal Day/time of delivery
Driver name	

Items To Be Sent:

Day/Date sent		Expected return	
For Whom	Item	Quantity	Special Instructions

Reminder List

shirts	skirts		
pants	blouses		
jackets	sweaters		
suits	jackets		
ties	dresses		
sweaters			

DIETARY NEEDS & FOOD FAVORITES

For:			Date:
Item	**Description**	**Dislikes**	**When Most Desired/Required**
Breakfast			
Lunch			
Dinner			
Snacks Always on Hand			
Comfort Foods Always on Hand			
Comfort Foods Occasional			
Beverages - Soft			
Beverages - Alcohol			
Special Foods for Guests			

DIETARY NEEDS & FOOD FAVORITES

For: **Date:**

Item	Description	Dislikes	When Most Desired/Required
Medications w/foods			
Meats			
Poultry/Game			
Fish			
Vegetables			
Fruits			
Grains			
Beverages			
Other			

WEEKLY MENU   WEEK

Monday	
Breakfast	
Snack	
Lunch	
Dinner	
Tuesday	
Breakfast	
Snack	
Lunch	
Dinner	
Wednesday	
Breakfast	
Snack	
Lunch	
Dinner	
Thursday	
Breakfast	
Snack	
Lunch	
Dinner	
Friday	
Breakfast	
Snack	
Lunch	
Dinner	
Prep for Next Day	

PARTY EVENT PLANNING

Event Host		Date
Theme		

Party Responsibilities	**Assigned**	**Comp**
1. Meet with parent and/or child for discussion about upcoming event.		
2. Meet with chef or caterer to discuss menu (unless hosts have decided).		
3. Send out invitation (preferably 3 weeks in advance). a. Hostess often calls first for informal chat.		
4. Review menu with chef or caterer to determine what items can be made ahead of time.		

5. Selection of theme, table cloths, china, crystal, silver, or whatever is to be used (be sure to check with hosts about selections).
    a. Be sure there are enough place settings - crystal, china, silver, etc.
    b. If enough not available, check with hosts for alternating patterns.		

6. Order and arrange flowers a day in advance so the blooms will be open. a. Think about combination of flowers and candles.		
7. Chef and florist should have an alternate plan in case they cannot find the necessary supplies.		
8. Make plans with housekeeper about the cleanliness of the house. Specifics for each room. (Check household Cleaning Standards for guidance.)		
9. Bathrooms are cleaned and stocked with any necessary item that guests might need.		

10. Check with hosts or the parents of the guests on any special needs.
    a. Dietary restrictions
    b. Food allergies
    c. Favorites
    d. Dislikes		

11. Arrange valet service to park cars if parents will be staying.		
12. Have a plan in case of inclement weather.		
13. Make sure that preparations are made to hang coats. Cards with names, places to store them, etc.		

PARTY EVENT PLANNING		
Event Host Theme		Date
Party Responsibilities	**Assigned**	**Comp**
14. Make arrangements for gifts for each child if this is the parent's wish.		
15. Snacks need to be set up around the room or house where the party is to take place. If a meal is planned it is best not to have snacks, or if so they should be light.		
16. Nanny to be aware of what is going on in the dining room at all times. a. Coordinate with chef about the time to serve if meal is being served or if only cake and snacks.		

17.   Serving and servers:
     a Feed servers and staff first.
     b. Servers should not be allowed to drink alcohol during dinner.
     c. Staff members should have change of clothes in case of spills.
     d. Servers are to be trained to the standard of the household.
     e. Good if you can train household staff to serve so they can be used in many different events.
     f. Servers are to use common sense and be mindful when serving. If they are removing from the right, but the guests are in conversation, they know that they DO NOT disturb, remove from the left. They try to anticipate the needs of the guest. (Check family Entertainment Standards.)		

19.   Clean-up:
     a. This is as important as the set up.
     b. House should be completely brought back to order before finished, no sign of the party should be left for the morning.
     c. Any spots on linens, furniture, carpet, etc. should be taken care of immediately.		

20. Record menu, guest list and theme in Nanny book.		
21. Give an oral/written report to hosts the next morning.		
22. Go over event with staff to discuss any changes necessary for future events.		

CHILDREN'S INVENTORY

Item	Brand Name	Inventory	Quantity Used Monthly
Diapers			
Baby powder			
Baby lotion			
Baby wipes			
A&D Ointment			
Zinc Oxide			
Soap			
Shampoo			
Kleenex			
Toilet tissue			
Bubble bath			
Cotton balls			
Vaseline			
Sun screen			
Aloe			
Children's Aspirin			
Cough Syrup			
Antiseptic ointment			
BandAids			
Ipecac- poison control			
Q-tips			
Combs			
Hair Bows etc.			

CHILDREN'S INVENTORY			
Item	**Brand Name**	**Inventory**	**Quantity Used Monthly**

TOY INFORMATION

Item

Description

Use or Age Restriction

Date Purchased / Cost

Storage Location

Serial Number

Disposition / Date

Notes

Toy Organization Chart

Item	Description	Use or age restrictions	Date purchased	Serial number	Original cost	Disposition

Closet Organization Chart

Item & Description	Style: Casual/Dress-up/Formal	Summer/Winter	Designer	Purchase Price	Disposition

Organization Chart For Shoes

	A	B	C	D	E	F	G	H	I
1									
2									
3									
4									
5									
6									
7									
8									
9									
10									
11									
12									

LIBRARY ORGANIZATION CHECKLIST

Books, Videos, Cassette Tapes, CDs, Computer Programs

Title	Media Format	Subject Matter	Copyright Date	Ownership

EXPENSE REPORT

Expenses Incurred by: Period Covered: From   To

Date	Description	Meals	Foods-Grocery	Transp. & Travel	Supplies	Enter-tainment	Other	Total
Totals								

	Cash Received in Advance	
Net amount due	
Date Received	

Notes:

Signature: Date:

Appendices

Appendix A

System Definitions

The Nanny Management System

is taken from the full **Starkey Household Management System** that is currently being utilized to set up households across the United States and Canada. This communication tool builds a *framework* or *blueprint* for service delivery to take place for the employer, the Nanny and the children. It paints a picture of how to promote a successful relationship with the parents for the care of children. It aids in creating clear communication between employers and Nannies, and helps to mutually decide how to manage the Nanny's time. This system adapts to any family, any service standard, all children, any home, and any position requirements.

The Environment

is the term the System uses to define where service to the children takes place; in most cases, your home. The environment includes the geographical and regional location, the property or estate, the people in the home, the size and style of the home, and the expenditure involved to maintain/improve the home and lifestyle.

Service Standards

are the ultimate goals of the household. It is the term we use to define the level of service being requested for the children, within the home environment, the image a given household and household members project. It is the children's and parents' specific styles and preferences. It is the *when* and *how* things are accomplished in the home. **The Starkey Household Management System** teaches that there are ten Service Standards and methodologies. These include standards for the following categories: Administrative, Grounds and Property, Maintenance, Cleaning, Cooking, Entertaining, Clothing, Security, Transportation and Travel, and Child Education or Elder Support.

Favorites

are the likes and dislikes of a particular family or family child member, such as a type or scent of flower, a style of food, needs due to allergies, the kind of toys or clothes they like, favorite friends, the schools they attend, etc. The daily living pattern of each child member of each household is unique. A Nanny Manager's ability to ascertain, anticipate and support these favorites is considered the *art form* of household service.

The Employer's Schedule

is an outline of the daily routine of the principals of the home. Most of us are creatures of habit. These habits may change, depending on the seasons or the home or whether house guests are present. The schedules are meant to get an idea of a typical day. What time do you get up, when do you work out, what time do you leave for work, what time is dinner, what do you like to do in the evenings, when do you go to bed? This schedule allows for the Nanny to schedule quality time for you with your children, to support your personal service needs and an overall children's schedule that will revolve around you.

Daily Graces

is the term Starkey uses for the tasks that provide the underlying daily structure and set the standards within a home. They are the duties that need to be done for the children and their home, which may include tasks such as making beds, picking up toys, feeding the pets, afternoon snacks, turning down beds in the evening, making a safety walk of the home and property in regards to the children and other traditions or gracious touches that surround the home and everyday lives of the children.

Day in the Life

is the phrase that Starkey uses to describe the daily household schedules and to report the everyday activities of the Nanny, the children, and even the employers. *The process of creating these schedules is essential to effective communication between the employer, the Nanny and the other household staff.* It outlines what the Nanny is doing. It helps clarify the daily pattern required of each employee. The **Day in the Life** schedules are time-oriented, listing the duties for each day with their approximate start and ending time for each employee.

Mastering the Moment

is the anticipation of, and readiness for *personal service*. Most Nanny Managers say it is the "fun and creative" piece of household management. To Master the Moment, the Nanny must have the childcare service delivery system fully functional. Use of the System enables the care of the children and home to be run from a pre-planned perspective, as opposed to a reactive or crisis mode. If a good structure of service delivery is in place, the children are always clean, the pantry is stocked with appropriate foods, transportation is always available and play time is safe so that schedules and time can be adequately changed to accommodate almost any unexpected request or event. **Moments are mastered**!

The Nanny Manager's Book

is the term we use for the notebook, binder, floppy disk, or other medium where every bit of information about your children and your service delivery system is organized and documented. It includes a description all of the aspects of setting up the household for the children's care and well being including the Environment, Service Standards, Favorites, Day in the Life, family recipes and children's menus, a list of the vendors, toy and clothing inventories, cleaning and maintenance task sheets, etc.

The Household Manager's Software

is a program designed to support the Starkey Household Management System and the Nanny Management System and it organizes your children's service delivery. It defines your childcare standards and favorites, your style of cleaning, Daily Graces, the children's schedule, and your Nanny's Day in the Life.

Appendix B

Nanny Search

Starkey International offers this useful information about the selection of Nannies to assist the family.

Starkey International has been actively recruiting and placing high-end Nannies since early 1981. We present a high standard of service, and quality candidates that have helped this industry grow. The search for "just the right Nanny" is very challenging and often time-consuming. It is imperative that our client identify the style and skill of Nanny that would best fit their individual needs. Starkey requires that position days are no more than 12 hours. We also request a minimum of a private room and private bath in a separate area of the home. Some families obtain a nearby apartment, if quarters are not available in the household.

Starkey requires that each of our clients fill out our Client Information Form. This form helps develop and identify the duties and parameters of the Nanny position. The Day in the Life section specifies exactly what a Nanny might do in an average day. It focuses the client's attention to the kind of structure initially required to set a daily schedule for the Nanny.

Starkey is helping to create and professionalize the Nanny role by sharing some of the information learned in our two decades of working in the household industry. Currently, the terminology is still inconsistent: our marketplace can use the term "Nanny" to describe anyone from an alien domestic to a highly-trained, experienced professional. The following will help you determine which level of Nanny is right for you.

☆ **The Domestic Helper**
This person is typically not well educated and not a decision-maker. For the most part, religion and family are important to them. They can be very good childcare providers, work long hours, and are quite flexible. However, these individuals are very difficult to

research and check out and often are not legal to work in this country. We recommend that these individuals be directly supervised. Salaries are typically $300/week and up. No experience or training is expected.

Note: Starkey does not recruit Domestic Helpers.

☆ Au Pair

A foreign national, typically a teenager, in the United States for up to one year to experience American life. Lives as a part of the host family and receives a small allowance/salary. Helps with housework and childcare. May or may not have prior childcare experience or training.

Note: Starkey does not recruit Au Pairs.

☆ Mother's Helper

Lives in or out and works for a family to provide full-time childcare and other domestic help for families with one parent at home most of the time. Usually works under direction and supervision of the at-home parent, but may be left in complete charge for brief periods. No special training is expected.

Note: Starkey does not recruit Mother's Helpers.

☆ The British Nursery Nurse

This British-trained Nanny is typically very structured and prefers to be "in charge." Many have attended a two-year Nanny training program and are taught the British style of caring for children (not limited to in-home care). These Nannies have passed the examination of the National Nursery Examination Board. They are committed to families, accept being "on call" and other requests found in the more aristocratic British style of household. If the cultural and childcare differences between the American and British home are sorted out, these Nannies are wonderful. Salaries typically start at $600/week plus separate housing. Be certain they are legal to work!

Note: Starkey recruits this level Nanny only if they are already accustomed to working in the U.S. and are currently legal to do so.

☆ The American "New" Nanny

Most are young (18 to 35) and have never learned how to live and work in a staffed household. The new Nanny requires training in household service etiquette. They are wonderful with children under five. Their self-esteem can be low and they are not always sophisticated in their thinking. They burn out quickly in on-call situations as little time is left for their personal lives. They do best in structured working-mom situations where they know what is expected. They are guided to set up basic play for toddlers, prepare simple children's lunches, and clean up children's toys where the parents are home before dinner. This level Nanny generally has some education (a few have been to Nanny schools and community college and are trained for the working-mother household). Salaries are typically $350/week and up.

Note: Starkey can provide short-term training for this level Nanny, but does not recruit them.

☆ The Career Nanny

This group (age 25 to 60) is very good at attending to the needs of young children, infants on up. As Nannies, they have gained personal and professional self-worth by having a sound footing in a particular child-development philosophy with which they have been successful. They are accustomed to having regular, set hours, and two consecutive full days off. There are enough families looking for them that they often choose an agency to represent them and have several position offerings. Their focus is on the children, not the housekeeping and cooking duties. Recent case law requires that when the Nanny is the responsible care giver, the Nanny's attention should not be divided with household chores. Most professional Nannies have learned to be flexible in their time, have some structure and are deeply committed to their families. These Nannies typically are expected to have experience and some college or continuing education in child development. Salaries are $500/week and up.

Note: Starkey generally represents this level Nanny.

☆ The Certified Nanny Manager

Once children enter school, a full-time Nanny is no longer needed. Families look for the professional who can pick up children after school, organize after-school activities, tutor, run errands, grocery shop, provide mature supervision and security while traveling, and pull together a basic evening meal following the family's favorite recipes. Salaries for these candidates are $600 per week and up. Training and experience are expected.

Note: Starkey trains and places this level person through our Starkey Nanny Advancement and Household Management Training Programs.

☆ **Governess**

Traditionally and educationally qualified, and certified teachers, this group is typically employed by families for full-time or at-home education of school-aged children. Teaches children and is not usually concerned with domestic work or the physical care of younger children. Hours of work and salaries are by arrangement.

Note: Starkey is able to recruit this professional.

Starkey has created the Starkey Nanny Advancement Program (S.N.A.P.), to address the continuing education needs of our Career Nannies and our Nanny employers. This 50-hour program teaches the Starkey Nanny Management System, understanding and competency regarding structuring a child's and Nanny's day, household etiquette, children's entertaining, safety and security procedures, travel issues, nutrition, and healthy, child-sensitive cooking.

For further information regarding the S.N.A.P. program or other educational programs and services offered, call Starkey at **1-877-STARKEY**.

APPENDIX C

<table>
<tr><td colspan="4" align="center">Formal Offer and Agreement</td></tr>
<tr><td colspan="2">From:
Date Submitted:</td><td colspan="2">To:
Date Returned:</td></tr>
<tr><td>Job Description
(See Client
Information
Form)</td><td colspan="3">You are being hired for your NANNY expertise.

This position will achieve success when the following are completed:
1. Service standards and organization of the Nanny duties within the household are identified and are organized in a Nanny Management plan to the satisfaction of the (fill in)_____________________ family. This includes "Day in the Life" schedules for both Nannies and children.

2. Nutritious meals and snacks are provided for the children of the household.

3. Management of the children, their activities and safety for the children are completed to the satisfaction of the family.

4. (Other)</td></tr>
<tr><td>Living Accom.
Salary /
Taxable
Income</td><td></td><td>Anticipated
Start Date</td><td></td></tr>
<tr><td>Hours/week</td><td></td><td>Living
Arrangements</td><td></td></tr>
<tr><td>Salary and
Performance
Reviews</td><td></td><td>Health
Benefits</td><td></td></tr>
<tr><td>Vacation
Allowed</td><td></td><td>Relocation
Expenses</td><td></td></tr>
<tr><td>Continuing
Education
Benefits</td><td colspan="3">We will provide a yearly allowance of $_______________ for the Starkey Nanny Advancement Program and/or other appropriate industry education.</td></tr>
<tr><td>Use of Car</td><td colspan="3">❑ For Household Use   ❑ For Personal Use   ❑ Both</td></tr>
<tr><td>Other</td><td colspan="3">This is a two-month trial period. At the end of two months, a performance review will be scheduled to mutually determine continuation of employment.</td></tr>
<tr><td colspan="4">Notes: As an employee, appropriate federal, state and social security taxes will be deducted from your paycheck. You are responsible for filing your own personal tax returns and paying any amounts due. We will provide appropriate W-2 forms at the end of each year.

Respectfully submitted by: I have read and agree with the information on this page:

___________________________   ___________________________</td></tr>
</table>

About the Author

The founder and President of The Starkey International Institute for Household Management, Inc., Mary Louise Starkey, has set the service standard by being at the forefront of the household service industry since 1981. As a granddaughter of one of the original Coca-Cola entrepreneurs, she has experienced both sides of the service relationship. Mrs. Starkey felt it was important to make her own mark rather than stay in her family's backyard. After striking out on her own, she became an ACTION volunteer working in the area of education and aging. She also earned a Bachelor of Science degree in Community Services Development. She married and gave birth to two sons, one now a comedian with Disney World and the other currently Marketing Director at Starkey. She is also a grandmother.

Mrs. Starkey is passionately devoted to what she does and strives to advance the industry, protect it and continue its growth. The Starkey Institute is the private industry's leader, developing standards of technical skills and professional ethics. Aside from promoting the prosperity of her own business, she is one of the founding members of the International Nanny Association, has served as a consultant in the start-up process for numerous placement firms, training schools and other service-oriented companies across the nation and serves as a lecturer and consultant to local businesses. She has also recently published two of a five-book series for the management of large homes, including *Mrs. Starkey's Nanny Manager* and *Setting Household Standards*. Mrs. Starkey's personal contribution to the industry has been hailed in such forums as *The New York Times, Los Angeles Times, USA Today, Cosmopolitan, Business Week* and on CBS Television's *Nightwatch*. She also serves many non-profits including the Zach Foundation, a group which serves the needs of burn victims, particularly children, and hosts four formal dinners per year that are devoted to raising funds to educate young adults who have been burned.

Mrs. Starkey is a true entrepreneur and an open-hearted visionary. She considers each of her graduates to be her children and, like any parent, she is passionately certain she knows best. Her ultimate vision is the creation of the profession of household management.

INDEX

More Ways to Bring the
Starkey Household Management System
to Your Home

Setting Household Standards

Setting up a service system in a large home requires a vision. Ultimately this vision is manifested in the look, the feel and the care of the home and of those who live within. *Setting Household Standards* helps you understand how to communicate your customized vision to your household staff. It gives you a structured organizational course of action for setting up your specific service standards, while developing service relationships with your staff. *Setting Household Standards* is ideal for use with *The Household Manager's Software*.

$129.00

The Household Manager's Software

A sophisticated relational data base created to support the service delivery functions within any household, this software provides the framework for structuring your household, allowing staff to become pro-active and more efficient. It documents your own personal Service Standards, manages events and inventories property, and most importantly, creates on-going cleaning and maintenance task sheets personalized to each day's specific needs. $650.00

Newsletters

Starkey Stars keeps the client informed about recent trends in the household industry and highlights graduates and veterans looking for placement in the household management industry. This newsletter is published four times a year.

$25/year

Tales from the Mansion is a quarterly publication designed for Household Service Professionals. It offers placement opportunities, articles of interest, recipes, and updates for and about Starkey graduates or those who have been placed by Starkey.

$25/year

Call Starkey at **1-877-STARKEY** (782-7539)
You may also order through our website at www.starkeyintl.com

Prices as of Fall 1998.

ORDER INFORMATION

Starkey & Associates, Inc.
1350 Logan Street
Denver, Colorado 80203

Toll free: 1-877-STARKEY
E-mail: products@starkeyintl.com
Website: www.starkeyintl.com

YES, I WOULD LIKE TO ORDER ONE OF YOUR PRODUCTS!

Product	# of copies	Price each
❏ *Setting Household Standards*		$129.00
❏ *The Household Manager's Software*		$650.00
❏ Software + *Setting Household Standards*		$695.00
❏ *Mrs. Starkey's Nanny Manager*		$79.95
❏ Additional Forms: Household Manager's Book		$15.00
❏ Additional Forms: Nanny Manager's Book		$15.00
❏ *Starkey Stars* Newsletter, for employers		$25.00
❏ *Tales from the Mansion* Newsletter, for Household Service Professionals		$25.00

❏ I am not interested in ordering at this time, please put
me on your mailing list for updates and future publications.

Name (Mr./Mrs./Ms.)

❏ Client

❏ Applicant

Mailing Address

City   State   Zip Code

Home Phone   Daytime Phone

Payment: ❏ check   ❏ money order   To pay by credit card, please complete: ❏ VISA   ❏ MASTERCARD

Account #   Expiration date

Valid Cardholder's Signature